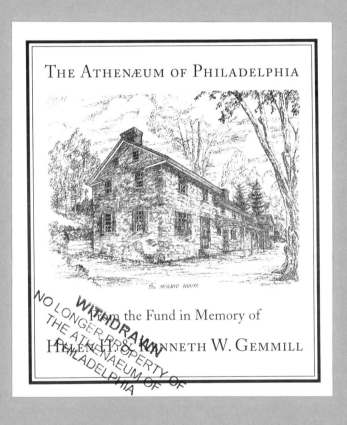

Philadelphia
MAESTROS

Philadelphia MAESTROS

ORMANDY, MUTI, SAWALLISCH

PHYLLIS WHITE RODRÍGUEZ-PERALTA

TEMPLE UNIVERSITY PRESS
Philadelphia

Temple University Press
1601 North Broad Street
Philadelphia PA 19122
www.temple.edu/tempress

Copyright © 2006 by Temple University
All rights reserved
Published 2006
Printed in the United States of America

Text design by Ox and Company, Inc.

⊗The paper used in this publication meets the requirements
of the American National Standard for Information
Sciences — Permanence of Paper for Printed Library
Materials, ANSI Z39.48-1992

Library of Congress Cataloging-in-Publication Data

Rodríguez-Peralta, Phyllis W.
        Philadelphia maestros : Ormandy, Muti,
Sawallisch / Phyllis White Rodríguez-Peralta.
                p. cm.
        Includes bibliographical references and index.
        ISBN 1-59213-487-4 (cloth : alk. paper)
        1. Conductors (Music) — Biography.
2. Ormandy, Eugene, 1899–1985. 3. Muti, Riccardo [1941–].
4. Sawallisch, Wolfgang, 1923– . 5. Philadelphia
Orchestra — History. I. Title.

ML402.R63 2006
784.2092'274811 — dc22
[B]
                                        2005054889

2   4   6   8   9   7   5   3   1

To the memory of my husband,
Lorenzo Rodríguez-Peralta, M.D.

CONTENTS

PREFACE

Loyal symphony audiences have always been fascinated by the musicians on stage, and particularly by the conductor who stands before the entire orchestra and shapes the music. He seems unerring, authoritative, powerful.

I am part of this loyal, music-loving audience, and from this perspective I have focused this book on the three past music directors of the Philadelphia Orchestra: Eugene Ormandy, Riccardo Muti, and Wolfgang Sawallisch. Although their professional lives are also tied to Europe, I have concentrated on the contributions of their years in Philadelphia. The three maestros are dissimilar in many ways – in personality, in conducting technique, in rehearsal policy, in repertoire and programming goals – yet they are alike in their complete dedication to their art.

In considering the role of the conductor, I have endeavored to probe the artistic and professional attributes of each of these music directors as well as the human factors bound up in their careers. The relationship between conductor and musicians is strangely contradictory; it is momentarily very close, particularly with principal players, but must also remain distant. The challenge for any conductor is to bring as many as a hundred or more musicians together to cooperate in a unified ensemble, and any partiality or particular friendship would be detrimental. Thus the conductor's working personality may differ from his natural personality.

Responsibility for the interpretation of the music belongs to the conductor, and the players must adhere to his will and adjust to his methods. Those of us sitting in the audience can appreciate the outer conformations of a conductor's interpretation, but we will probably not be able to hear all the subtleties that can be attributed to a particular conductor. Even an orchestra member who happened to be in the audience for a particular performance might not recognize every nuance and shading. As one musician said to me, you have to be within the music to detect all the subtleties and differences that are the results of the conductor's concept. But they are always there.

At times, to illustrate certain comparisons, I have mentioned the conductors on either side of the three maestros, Stokowski before Ormandy, and Eschenbach after Sawallisch. There seems to be an alternating pattern in their appointments. The tempestuous Stokowski, a consummate showman, was followed by the outwardly unassuming Ormandy, who could forge amiable relations with the board of directors. The dramatic, exciting Muti was followed by the dignified, formal Sawallisch, the embodiment of Old World refinement. Eschenbach gives evidence of a return to showmanship, but of a different kind. Stokowski, Ormandy, and Muti were in their thirties when they assumed their posts with the Philadelphia Orchestra. Sawallisch and Eschenbach are mature conductors who have proved themselves with other major orchestras. Each of these maestros was trained in a principal instrument: Stokowski in organ, Ormandy in violin, and Muti, Sawallisch, and Eschenbach in piano. Some say that each conductor's approach to an orchestra reflects his particular instrument.

Everyone has heard about the "Philadelphia sound," a phrase that usually refers to the lushness of the strings and is associated particularly with Ormandy. This "sound," however, really varies according to the conductor, the composer, and the venue. The seeds were sown by Stokowski, flowered with Ormandy, were strictly cultivated by Muti, and flowered again, but with more definition, under Sawallisch. Eschenbach's influence is just beginning. In this book I discuss the changes that occurred under the batons of Ormandy, Muti, and Sawallisch, for the sound is transformed according to the conductor's wishes. It is always his orchestra.

The Philadelphia Orchestra has been fortunate in the continuity of its conductors, counting only six through the twentieth century, with the seventh arriving near the beginning of the twenty-first. November 16, 1900, is the

Orchestra's birth date. Fritz Scheel served as its first music director until his death in 1907. Next came Carl Pohlig (from 1907 until his resignation in 1912), followed by Leopold Stokowski (1912 to 1938). Eugene Ormandy served as co-conductor from 1936 until 1938 and held the post of music director until 1980. Riccardo Muti became the music director in 1980, serving until 1992, and Wolfgang Sawallisch was the music director from 1993 to 2003. Christoph Eschenbach assumed the directorship in September 2003. All were Europeans: Scheel and Pohlig were German; Stokowski was born in London of a Polish father; Ormandy was a Hungarian who became an American citizen; Muti is Italian; Sawallisch and Eschenbach are German.

The Orchestra itself has become quite international in its makeup and has shifted from the initial predominance of European players to Americans, with the recent addition of Asian and Latin American musicians. The fact that so many musicians are trained in the Curtis Institute of Music contributes to its cohesion. Playing together are fathers and sons, brothers, husbands and wives, teachers and former students.

Ormandy, Muti, and Sawallisch faced many ordeals in their respective tenures – economic difficulties, strikes, upheavals with the board, difficult personnel, recording cancellations, disagreements over leaving the

Orchestra's original home in the Academy of Music. Over all these problems looms the graying of the audience. The chauffeured limousines with matrons from the Main Line may have disappeared, but they have been replaced by lines of buses from retirement communities. What concerns everyone is the necessity of attracting new and younger audiences, and each of the three conductors has proposed solutions.

Philadelphia audiences owe a debt of gratitude to the three music directors who guided the Orchestra during 66 years. In spite of the anxiety inherent today in all symphony orchestras, the Philadelphia Orchestra continues to be one of the greatest in the world.

A NOTE ON SOURCES

The research for this book has taken several forms. In addition to the usual published sources, including the archives of the Philadelphia Orchestra and the holdings of specialized music libraries, I have relied on personal interviews with many members of the Orchestra. The musicians made certain requests in exchange for candor: some agreed to allow their names to appear in the Acknowledgments, but preferred not to be quoted in the text; others wanted complete anonymity. In Chapter Four, each soloist read the questions and answers of the interview in their final form before it was submitted for publication.

ACKNOWLEDGMENTS

I wish to express my gratitude to the many musicians of the Philadelphia Orchestra who shared their time and thoughts with me, in particular those who have played under the batons of all three maestros: William de Pasquale, co-concertmaster; Richard Woodhams, principal oboist; Lloyd Smith, acting associate principal cellist; Ronald Reuben, bass clarinetist; and Jerome Wigler, violinist; as well as David Kim, concertmaster, who joined the Orchestra in 1999. I am indebted also to the artists who added their personal concepts of the maestros in the chapter entitled "Voices from the Music World": Gary Graffman, Lang Lang, and Sarah Chang.

In addition, I want to thank Joanne Barry, archivist of the Orchestra, and John Pollack, public services specialist of the Rare Book and Manuscript Library of the University of Pennsylvania, for their assistance. Nicholas Saunders, director of concert operations at the Juilliard School, facilitated my contacts with the managements of the soloists whom I interviewed.

I am especially grateful to my daughter Carmen, who was my consultant and who contributed her musical knowledge as a pianist as well as her constant encouragement.

I also wish to thank Micah Kleit, Executive Editor of the Temple University Press, for his invaluable help, as well as Jennifer French, Senior Production Editor, and Jane Barry, my copy editor, for their meticulous work.

(previous) Eugene Ormandy conducting the Orchestra. Courtesy of the University of Pennsylvania Rare Book and Manuscript Library

ᘒ Eugene Ormandy ᘓ

The Friday afternoon audience on October 30, 1931, waited expectantly for the idolized Arturo Toscanini to stride onto the stage. Instead, they watched with amazement as a diminutive, very young-looking conductor with reddish hair, unknown to most of them, ascended the podium. This was Eugene Ormandy's first appearance at the Academy of Music, an unexpected debut that led eventually to 44 years of his leadership of the Philadelphia Orchestra.

Toscanini had been engaged as guest conductor for two weeks of concerts, but shortly before the first rehearsal he cabled from Italy that a bout of neuritis in his right arm would prevent his arrival. The Orchestra's manager, Arthur Judson, frantically approached many major conductors to substitute for Toscanini, but no one accepted. Some had previous commitments, but others surely declined because they did not want to be compared with the adulated Toscanini, or with the equally famous

Leopold Stokowski, the music director of the Philadelphia Orchestra, who was on vacation. Ormandy was the only one available. In spite of being warned that it might be a disastrous move, Ormandy accepted the risk.

The scheduled program was not an easy one: Brahms's Symphony No. 4 in E Minor, Op. 98; Jaromir Weinberger, Polka and Fugue from *Schwanda*; Strauss, *Till Eulenspiegel* and Waltzes from *Rosenkavalier*. And there were only three days before the first rehearsal! Ormandy memorized everything over the weekend. On Monday he took the train from New York, where he was living, to Philadelphia and began rehearsing with the Orchestra. He conducted the program on the following Friday afternoon.

The critics and the audience were unanimous in their praise of his absolute authority over the music. His success even became national news. Judson, who had prudently waited to see the results of this challenge, offered him the second week of substituting for Toscanini.

Ormandy's good fortune continued. The Minneapolis Symphony Orchestra (now called the Minnesota Symphony) was placed in an impossible situation when its conductor, Henri Verbrugghen, suffered an incapacitating stroke. The orchestra manager, having read the newspaper reports about this Ormandy "who was good enough to substitute for Toscanini," desperately phoned a Minneapolis lawyer, Willis Norton, who happened to be in Philadelphia. She asked him to attend one of Ormandy's concerts and form an opinion of the young conductor. Norton was present for the following Saturday night concert and called back to say that Ormandy was wonderful. Judson was contacted and arrangements were made for Ormandy to leave immediately for Minneapolis when he finished his engagement in Philadelphia. After his final, very successful Saturday night performance, Ormandy boarded the night train for Minnesota. His first rehearsal with that orchestra went well; in fact, the musicians stood and applauded. After the second rehearsal, the board of directors signed him to a five-year contract.

The Minneapolis Symphony at that time was a fairly respectable orchestra in the Midwest, but it was certainly not one of America's great orchestras. In his few years with the orchestra, Ormandy transformed it into an excellent symphony ensemble. He persuaded, cajoled, goaded, and endlessly drilled the musicians. He brought in new personnel, introduced more extensive repertoire with new twentieth-century works, and began tours throughout the Midwest, often under trying conditions. Because the orchestra was in debt during these depression years, he instituted "Viennese Afternoons," which were very popular. He became a civic leader of sorts and appeared at any function that would benefit the orchestra.

Technicians from RCA Victor came to Minneapolis for two weeks in 1934, and again for two weeks in 1935. Within this timeframe the orchestra recorded every day for six hours. More than a hundred works resulted, and for a while the Minneapolis Orchestra was the most recorded symphony orchestra in the United States. Although neither Ormandy nor the orchestra members received royalties, the recordings brought prestige and recognition to both the orchestra and Ormandy himself.

During these years Ormandy appeared several times as guest conductor of the Philadelphia Orchestra, where he was always greeted with special affection by the Philadelphia audiences. When Stokowski decided in 1936 to withdraw as full-time director of the Philadelphia Orchestra, Ormandy became the natural choice for the position of co-conductor. The board's decision was acceptable to Stokowski, who had recommended three names for the position: Carlos Chávez, José Iturbi, and Eugene Ormandy. Ormandy would conduct for 22 weeks, and Stokowski for six. There were some months left on Ormandy's contract with the Minneapolis Orchestra, but its board of directors, grateful for all he had done for that orchestra, graciously released him.

Relations between Ormandy and Stokowski remained amicable during their shared conductorship. This was principally due to Ormandy's patience and his ability to defer to his flamboyant co-conductor. For example, Ormandy chose his programs after Stokowski had decided what he wanted to conduct. At one point Stokowski referred to the "delightful friendship between Mr. Ormandy and myself [which] is unusual between conductors."[1] The two did differ on the arrangement of the orchestra sections, for Stokowski put the strings behind the brass, woodwinds, and percussion; Ormandy moved them to their usual positions when he was conducting. Another difference concerned the manner of bowing in the violins: Stokowski permitted free bowing, while Ormandy, a violinist, preferred uniform bowing.

After two years as co-conductor, Ormandy became the music director of the Philadelphia Orchestra, a post desired by many world-renowned conductors. Stokowski would maintain the same connection with the Orchestra. His turbulent association with the board of directors had occasioned several proffered resignations, which then were withdrawn. In March 1941, after his relations with the board had further deteriorated, Stokowski announced his final resignation.

Pessimists predicted that the Orchestra would never survive without Stokowski, let alone maintain its excellent reputation. They favored engaging a conductor with extensive experience and a charismatic personality. Although Ormandy had fine European training as a violinist, as a conductor he had relatively limited experience, especially to be named music director of an Orchestra considered by many to be the finest symphony orchestra in America. But the board of directors emphasized the economics of the situation. A conductor of Stokowski's stature would mean a correspondingly high salary, and after eight years of deficits, this situation needed to be taken into account. Ormandy's salary was considerably lower. Moreover, the board wanted someone who would consider the audiences' preference for familiar music and institute the type of programming that might augment ticket sales. Ormandy was the opposite of a celebrity conductor; he was completely dedicated to this one Orchestra; and his appointment held the promise of a smooth relationship with the board.

On September 28, 1938, Ormandy received the official title of music director of the Philadelphia Orchestra, with "full authority over the orchestra's personnel, the content of programs, and the selection of soloists and guest conductors."[2]

Eugene Ormandy (Jenö Blau) was born in Budapest, Hungary, on November 18, 1899. His father named him Jenö (Eugene in English) in honor of Hungary's greatest violinist, Jenö Hubay; the conductor himself would change his last name to Ormandy.[3] His father was a dentist whose ambition had been to be a violinist, and he was determined that his son would be a violin virtuoso. A precocious child, Jenö, before he was two, could identify many compositions after only a few bars; at three he was reading music; at four he was studying violin with his stern father, on a one-eighth-size violin made especially for him. That he possessed perfect pitch is illustrated by a frequently repeated story: as a very young child, he was taken to a violin recital, and from his seat he shouted, "You played F sharp instead of F natural." (Some versions say, "F natural instead of F sharp.") At five-and-a-half, he was the youngest student ever admitted to the Royal Academy of Music in Budapest. He made his concert debut at age seven. At nine he entered the violin master classes of Jenö Hubay, after whom he had been named, and he studied composition with Zoltán Kodály. Just before he turned 14, he received an artist's diploma, and at 17, with a professor's certificate, he became the youngest person ever to teach violin at the Royal Academy.

In addition to his academy studies, he practiced three to four hours a day at home, until, he says, his fingers were numb. His taskmaster father kept rigorous control over his progress, and, in fact, was never convinced that his son's subsequent career as a conductor was the equal of being a violin virtuoso. A later episode illustrates his father's intransigent ambition for his son. In 1935 a magnificent

Eugene Ormandy as a young violinist on tour in Europe before his arrival in the United States in 1921. Courtesy of the University of Pennsylvania Rare Book and Manuscript Library

international concert was given for the Eucharistic Congress held in Budapest. Joseph Szigeti was guest violinist and Jenö Hubay was host. Eugene Ormandy, conductor of the Minneapolis Symphony Orchestra at that point, was asked to conduct. All that his father could say, tearfully, after the concert was, "If I had only disciplined you more severely, you might have been in Szigeti's place tonight."[4]

In 1917 Ormandy began his studies in philosophy at the University of Budapest. In that same year he became the concertmaster and soloist with the Blüthner Orchestra and toured Germany and Hungary. Later he concertized in Austria, France, and central Europe. Meanwhile Hubay had resigned from the Royal Academy, and Ormandy took his place. He was not very successful, however, because others on the faculty resented his youth.

At one point, two so-called concert agents (some say it was only one) proposed a contract for 100 concerts in the United States for a total of $30,000. Thinking of the famous, well-paid European violinists in America, Ormandy jumped at the chance. He sold everything to pay for his voyage and, almost penniless, arrived in New York on December 2, 1921. The promoters turned out to be amateurs who had no idea how to proceed in America. The contract was worthless, and since nothing could be arranged without money up front, the promoters disappeared.

Ormandy was alone in New York with no money, no job, and very little command of English. How he wound up in the Capitol Theater Orchestra has several versions. According to one, he remembered meeting a Hungarian friend in one of the many management offices that he and his agents had visited unsuccessfully. He went back to the office, obtained the man's address, and contacted him. This friend suggested that he present himself to Erno Rapee, music director of the Capitol Theater Orchestra. A more dramatic version has Ormandy standing on the corner of 50th and Broadway, with only a few cents in his pocket, when an acquaintance from Budapest bumped into him. He gave Ormandy a loan and advised him to see Erno Rapee, a native of Budapest, who held an important music position at the Capitol Theater, a silent movie house. (Still another version has Erno Rapee himself as the acquaintance.) Whatever the details, the important thing is that Ormandy was hired for the last row of the violin section. Within a week he was promoted to concertmaster. For two and a half years, four times a day, and every day of the week, he performed in this capacity, and he memorized his own parts and those of the other musicians as well. There were no thoughts of becoming a conductor.

Unexpected changes came suddenly. One day in 1924, the current conductor, David Mendoza, fell ill. Ormandy was given 15 minutes' notice to take over the conducting. The orchestra was playing a movement from Tchaikovsky's Fourth Symphony, which Ormandy had already memorized; consequently, he conducted without a score. His performance was so successful that he became an alternate assistant conductor as well as concertmaster, and in 1925-26, when two conductors left, he became the full-time associate conductor. He also played violin solos on a weekly radio program that originated in the Capitol Theater.

His friends kept telling him that it was madness to devote his talents to motion-picture-theater music. But since the orchestra often played classical music before the silent film began, Ormandy was acquiring an extensive repertoire. In addition, as they performed every work more than twenty times in succession, Ormandy said that it gave him "an almost incomparable opportunity to learn the music with intensive minuteness."[5] In his spare time he kept on memorizing new scores and attending symphony concerts. And he began to follow assiduously Toscanini's rehearsals at Carnegie Hall.

Word began to spread about the fine performances of the Capitol Theater Orchestra. The well-known concert manager Arthur Judson appeared at one of these performances. He listened and watched Ormandy carefully. He also heard Ormandy conduct an orchestra at Carnegie Hall that was made up in large part of musicians from the

New York Philharmonic. (The occasion was a dance recital given by Anna Duncan, the adopted daughter of Isadora Duncan.) Convinced of his potential, Judson offered a contract to the young Ormandy with the plan of developing him into a symphonic conductor. Ormandy resigned from the Capitol Theater in 1929.

At the beginning of their association, Judson had Ormandy conducting orchestra concerts on several regular radio broadcasts. In the summer of 1927, he placed him as the guest conductor of the New York Philharmonic at Lewisohn Stadium in New York, and in the summer of 1930 as guest conductor of the Philadelphia Orchestra for three concerts at the Robin Hood Dell in Philadelphia's Fairmount Park. The next summer Ormandy was invited back to the Robin Hood Dell for seven concerts.

It is to Ormandy's credit that, from the first, he never attempted to imitate Stokowski in spite of his admiration for his spectacular co-conductor. With confidence in his own abilities, Ormandy remained himself, an unostentatious conductor whose aim was to produce beautiful music, not the creation of a celebrity personality. There were no podium dramatics, for he was not a showman in any way. The audiences saw a mild, confident leader whom they liked.

Within the Orchestra, the atmosphere was very different. Ormandy was probably the last of the dictatorial conductors, and he remained a rigorous taskmaster. With his authoritative approach to the Orchestra, the musicians always knew that he considered them players who needed to be formed by him.

Ormandy's initial years as music director were often clouded by the public's continuing fascination with Stokowski. In 1939, after a 15-month absence, Stokowski returned to the Orchestra for three weeks. Music critics in Philadelphia and New York lauded the splendor, the sonority, the brilliance of color, and other qualities that they stated were possible only with Stokowski.

During this transitional period, there was unrest in the Orchestra itself. Two players resigned, a first violinist and a trombonist, who said that they missed the inspiration of Stokowski. Others criticized Ormandy's dismissal of the principal cellist, Isidore Gusikoff, for insubordination. (The cellist attributed his firing to Ormandy's perception that he had played better for Stokowski.) At a Friday afternoon concert, Stokowski defended Ormandy to the audience by saying that the players were performing magnificently and that under Ormandy they had fine guidance.[6] Subsequently the Orchestra members and the board supported Ormandy in public statements. After 1941, when Stokowski had definitely left the Philadelphia scene, Ormandy emerged in his own right.

The musicians respected Ormandy's prodigious memory, his infallible ear, and his intuitive musicianship. Yet Ormandy was not the easiest conductor to follow because he was usually imprecise in his indications, preferring, instead, more general signals. He used a style of conducting which did not dictate a distinct and simultaneous beginning attack by all the instrumental sections, but one which, in the Academy of Music, would roll through the Orchestra and be heard as a cohesive sound in the hall. In addition, he was more interested in elongating a phrase than in precise rhythm.

Ormandy soon discovered that the Academy, home of the Philadelphia Orchestra, had its acoustical peculiarities, and he took rehearsal time to go out and sit in various spots of the Academy in order to judge the sound from the audience's point of view. It can be said that Ormandy geared his conducting to the acoustics of the Academy. As a violinist he was, of course, string-oriented. The famous "Philadelphia sound," which over the years became a mantra to describe the Orchestra, refers to tonal beauty, to a resplendent sound that comes particularly from the strings.[7] The tone is rich, glowing, luxurious. On this point the normally unassuming Ormandy was adamant. "The Philadelphia sound? The Philadelphia sound is me."[8]

To produce the brilliance and lushness that he wanted, Ormandy insisted that the strings play strenuously. For more sonority he often had the second violins play in the same register as the first violins. Preferring a higher pitch, he wanted the Orchestra to be tuned to A442 rather than the usual A440 or A441. Sometimes he changed the instrumentation of a composition: for example, having the contrabassoon double the bass clarinet, or giving parts to the trumpets or trombones to augment the horns. He edited and cut the music, making personal inserts, even in well-known works. This was accomplished by taping strips of music paper over the original scores. (Hundreds of these inserts were kept in envelopes and used when Ormandy conducted, then removed for guest conductors.) Obviously Ormandy was not a purist or a music historian, and he was not concerned with the "authenticity" that has come to be seen as essential today, particularly in early music. His approach to music was uncomplicated: music was for enjoyment, even for entertainment.

Ormandy stood quite still on the podium, without much body motion and without moving his feet. The soaring climaxes that he could produce came from increasing his arm gestures. He used a baton for the first two years with the Orchestra until he tore a ligament in his right shoulder, which necessitated surgery. Following his doctors' orders, he began to limit his use of the baton, with certain exceptions, such as his appearance in the orchestra pit of the Metropolitan Opera in 1950, when the singers said they could not see his beat from their positions on stage. Ormandy's hands were especially expressive. Sometimes in rehearsals he illustrated the effect he wanted by seeming to be playing the violin, although he never picked up a violin to play a passage. Ormandy's memory was so extraordinary that he preferred to conduct without a score, except for concertos and new works.

He did not always bring in a player at the correct time, but this became the player's fault, not his. Such mistakes brought furious glances from him, but no one dared to question him about his cues. He was known to stare fixedly at a particular Orchestra player who displeased him, to the point of disturbing the player's concentration.

Ormandy's method of auditioning players for the Orchestra reflected the accepted procedures of his day. There were no committees, and Ormandy was present for all auditions, not just the final one. He sat in the hall with his back to the players so as not to be influenced by appearance. And he instructed the rehearsal pianist to change rhythms deliberately in order to judge how well the player was able to follow.

The changes that Ormandy made in the orchestral personnel came gradually, as he preferred to wait for normal attrition. Although he was reluctant to fire anyone outright, he did move the musicians around within their sections if they stopped measuring up to his standards, a harsh practice that was unorthodox and greatly disliked by the musicians. For many years there was a compulsory retirement age of 65, and over time the Stokowski players left and were replaced, often by young musicians from the Curtis Institute of Music in Philadelphia. By 1968-69, only eight players remained who had been hired by Stokowski. Like Stokowski before him, Ormandy slowly began to hire women musicians; there were six women in the Orchestra by 1944, and eight by 1966. In the 1938-39 season, Nadia Boulanger conducted two concerts and thus became the first woman to lead the Orchestra.

Ormandy's repertoire ran the gamut of musical styles and periods, but he placed special emphasis on music from the Romantic era, in which he excelled. Favorite works from this period were usually repeated on a cycle of four years or so. Ormandy also played new twentieth-century music, although, at the beginning of his tenure, less than Stokowski and more conservatively chosen out of consideration for the audience's taste. He always tried to balance new works with audience favorites, and he never closed a concert with an unknown composition. His twentieth-century choices ranged from post-Romantic to the avant-garde: Bela Bartók, Paul Hindemith, Zoltán Kodály, Sergei Prokofiev, Samuel Barber, Gian Carlo Menotti,

Walter Piston, Benjamin Britten, Howard Hanson, Igor Stravinsky, Vincent Persichetti, Roger Sessions, Randall Thomson, Dmitri Shostakovich, Kryzsztof Penderecki, Heitor Villa Lobos, and Alberto Ginastera were some of the composers whom he favored and whose names are now well-known.

Ormandy's involvement in world and U.S. premieres deserves praise. He himself conducted 96 world premieres and 44 U.S. premieres. Of special note are his world premieres of Bartók's Piano Concerto No. 3, BB 127, and Rachmaninoff's *Symphonic Dances,* and the American premieres of Shostakovich's Fourth, Thirteenth, and Fourteenth symphonies.

Sergei Rachmaninoff, in 1940, offered Ormandy the first performance of his *Symphonic Dances.* After the initial rehearsal, he turned to the musicians and said: "Today, when I think of composing, my thoughts turn to you, the greatest orchestra in the world. For that reason, I dedicated this, my newest composition, to the members of the Philadelphia Orchestra and to your conductor, Eugene Ormandy."[9]

The Philadelphia composer Vincent Persichetti said: "There is virtually no one who will put so much of his heart into seeing that a new work gets off on the right foot . . . insists on memorizing the composition and discussing it with you from every aspect. He invites you to rehearsals and has you sit alongside him. You are invited to interrupt at any time, to say whether something should be played faster, slower, or whether something is wanting in dynamics. Any suggestion gets his courteous consideration. It all contributes by giving the writer an inner satisfaction, a feeling that he not only has had his work played by the greatest orchestra of them all, but he has found the best possible performance that the orchestra could have given it."[10]

Ormandy had tremendous success when he and his Orchestra accompanied soloists, particularly instrumentalists. He was very flexible with soloists, which allowed a degree of spontaneity, and he was always able to anticipate and collaborate perfectly with them. All the great performers appeared with Ormandy and the Philadelphia Orchestra. Pianists Arturo Rubinstein and Rudolf Serkin became particular friends who performed often with him. Artists as diverse as Gary Graffman, Alicia de Larrocha, Radu Lupu, Maurizio Pollini, Van Cliburn, André Watts, Fritz Kreisler, Efrem Zimbalist, Isaac Stern, Itzhak Perlman, Pinchas Zuckerman, Mstislav Rostropovitch, Kirsten Flagstad, Lauritz Melchior, Marian Anderson, Beverly Sills, Plácido Domingo, and Luciano Pavarotti praised his conscientious preparation and sensitive support. Ormandy was respectful to established musicians, especially superstars. In addition, appearances with

Ormandy conducting. Courtesy of the University of Pennsylvania Rare Book and
Manuscript Library

Ormandy and the Philadelphia Orchestra helped the careers of many young soloists.

Sergei Rachmaninoff, another fast friend, appeared in 1939 as soloist in two concerts and as conductor in one other. As soloist, he had requested a 90-minute rehearsal. However, he did not ask for a repeat of any passage, and the rehearsal was finished in a half-hour. Rachmaninoff said that this was the first time he had not needed to go over any part of the concerto. The incident illustrates once more the thorough and detailed preparation that Ormandy brought to every performance.

The violinist David Oistrakh made his debut with the Philadelphia Orchestra in November 1955. He was so pleased with Ormandy and the Orchestra that he wrote his praise in a Soviet newspaper: "There is hardly another orchestra in the world which may be compared in beauty of tone, flexibility, harmonious ensemble, and abundance of variety, nuances and color. It is very difficult to imagine that anyone else could fit in as conductor for this orchestra except Eugene Ormandy."[11]

Ormandy was unique among conductors, not only because of his long tenure of 44 years with the Philadelphia Orchestra, but because he preferred to center his conducting on this one orchestra instead of traveling constantly for other engagements or combining conductorships, which had become the vogue. He spoke openly of the advantages of continuity, both to the orchestra and to the conductor, and he stressed the increased rapport that he felt grows between the members of the orchestra and a conductor with undivided loyalty.

Ormandy's complete dedication to the Philadelphia Orchestra meant that there were fewer guest conductors compared with other symphony orchestras, although many outstanding guest conductors were invited throughout the years. Among these were Dimitri Mitropoulos, George Szell, Igor Stravinsky, Zoltán Kodály, Leonard Bernstein, William Steinberg, Claudio Abbado, Rafael Frühbeck de Burgos, Carlo María Giulini, Lorin Maazel, Seiji Ozawa, and, of special interest, Wolfgang Sawallisch (Philadelphia debut in 1966) and Riccardo Muti (Philadelphia debut in 1972).

Ormandy believed that a conductor whose roots are in his community should make himself and his orchestra an integral part of that community. Accordingly, he and the Orchestra were present for many of Philadelphia's celebrations. Festivities were often held in large department stores, such as Wanamaker's or Gimbel's. During World War II the Orchestra visited local USO clubs and played pieces judged to be appropriate, from "Smoke Gets in Your Eyes" to the "Toreador's Song" from the opera *Carmen*. Ormandy was creative in finding ways for the Orchestra to appear in unexpected circumstances. In

April 1952, when the Broad Street Station of the Pennsylvania Railroad was slated for demolition, Ormandy and the Orchestra, on their way to a spring tour, were on the final train to leave the station. Before they left, Ormandy, from the platform, led the Orchestra's brass in "Auld Lang Syne" and the entire Orchestra, plus a huge crowd, in "The Star Spangled Banner."

In accord with his adherence to local involvement, he often used the Temple University Concert Choirs for choral works with the Orchestra. The students, whom he treated as he did the Orchestra members, were somewhat cowed by his presence. At one rehearsal, a young freshman was assigned to play the piano reduction of the orchestra part. Uncertain of Ormandy's manner of conducting, she entered incorrectly. Ormandy immediately stopped the music and reproved the pianist. (One of the assistant conductors, who was sitting next to the piano, whispered to her that no one was ever sure of Ormandy's downbeats.) After the rehearsal had ended, Ormandy complimented the pianist on her octaves.

As one of his contributions to the Philadelphia music scene, Ormandy taught classes in conducting at the Curtis Institute of Music. He was listed as a member of the faculty, but he gave his salary to Curtis.

The summer season at the Robin Hood Dell in Philadelphia's Fairmount Park was an integral part of the

Orchestra's life. In addition, after the 1963 contract gave the musicians 52 weeks of work a year, the Orchestra in 1966 added a three-week residency during August at the Saratoga Performing Arts Center in upstate New York. Guest conductors were invited now and then, but following his custom of full dedication to the Orchestra, Ormandy conducted the majority of these summer concerts.

New York provided maximum exposure in the music world. It was during the Ormandy era that the Philadelphia Orchestra began to sponsor its own Carnegie Hall subscription series, which has continued until the present.

On the other hand, Ormandy was opposed to permitting time off for outside chamber music or solo performances. As he gave his complete devotion to the Orchestra, he expected the same from the musicians. (Today a player is expected, even encouraged, to perform outside the Orchestra.)

The Philadelphia Orchestra is probably the most widely traveled orchestra in the world. Ormandy believed strongly in tours, both national and international, and the board highly approved of these tours because of the perceived economic benefits of the exposure. The musicians themselves did not always share this enthusiasm because of the extensive time away from their families.

In May 1949 the Orchestra had its first important foreign tour. Traveling by ship to England, they gave

28 concerts in 27 days. The presenters in the cities on the tour could choose among 20 programs consisting of 70 works. Ormandy programmed many American compositions, but, by agreement, British music was excluded. In Manchester so many wanted to attend the concert that they had to schedule a second performance. Over ten thousand attended the final concert in London's Harringay Arena, and almost five thousand were turned away. Obviously the trip was a great success, with the exception of a few critical remarks. One critic[12] advanced his idea of the reason for the Orchestra's outstanding beauty in performance – money! Money to pay for the best musicians, money for the finest instruments, and money to pay the conductor a movie star's salary. The *London Times* had high praise for the Orchestra, but slipped in a rare criticism of Ormandy by suggesting that he did not always get beneath the surface of the music. This disparagement was offset by other critiques. Sir Thomas Beecham, who conducted one tour concert, was especially complimentary: "Of all the American orchestras I have conducted in recent years, yours is by far the greatest. It has beauty of tone, youthful enthusiasm, exquisite balance."[13]

In 1955 the Orchestra traveled by air to Europe and concertized in France, Belgium, the Netherlands, Spain, Portugal, Italy, Switzerland, Austria, West Germany, Sweden, and Finland. (In Finland they met the 89-year-old

Jean Sibelius, whose music they had often played.) In 1958 it was Europe again. This time the tour spanned 14 countries, including a return to England and concerts in the Soviet Union and countries behind the Iron Curtain. The highlight of their 1970 tour of Europe was Ormandy's "discovery," in Florence, of the young Riccardo Muti. Their 1975 tour of Europe took them to six countries over a four-week period. They played 20 concerts in 17 cities, and Ormandy conducted every one of these concerts. In June 1966 there was a 10-nation tour of Latin America, sponsored by the State Department. There were three tours of Japan, in 1967, 1972, and 1978, the last of which included South Korea. In every foreign concert, Ormandy always programmed at least one American work.

The 1973 tour was the most publicized because it was the first time that an American symphony orchestra had performed in China. The tour resulted from a personal request by President Nixon, who had made his historic visit to China in the previous year. In China the Orchestra gave seven concerts in nine days. Ormandy was invited by the regular conductor to rehearse the Central Philharmonic Orchestra of Peking (now Beijing), and he received lavish praise for the expertise of his suggestions and guidance.

The Philadelphia Orchestra was Ormandy's whole life, and he had few other interests. Even on tours he rarely did any sightseeing, but preferred to stay in his room and study scores. The exception was this tour to China, where he visited the Great Wall and other places of interest.

The foreign tours were more dramatic, but the domestic tours were equally important. During the World War II years, the Orchestra was necessarily restricted to trips close to home. They played in various parts of the South and in New York, Baltimore, Washington, and Harrisburg. Once in Savannah, Georgia, the train was so late that there was no time to change and the musicians had to play in their wrinkled clothes. In Richmond, Virginia, Ormandy spotted in the audience a former violinist of the Orchestra who had been drafted. He invited the GI, in uniform, to conduct Sousa's *The Stars and Stripes Forever*.[14] After the war the Orchestra was able to do more extensive touring, beginning in 1946 with a 42-day tour across the United States and into Canada. From then on, there were constant trips throughout the United States.

Leopold Stokowski had been in the audience for the concert in Kiev during the Orchestra's 1958 tour; it was the second day of his own rehearsal with the Ukrainian State Orchestra. He had not heard the Philadelphia Orchestra for 17 years, from the final time that he had resigned from the Orchestra. After the Kiev meeting, he received an invitation from the board to conduct in Philadelphia during the 1959-60 season. A press release stated that Stokowski was returning "at the invitation of Eugene Ormandy." (Opinions differ as to whether it was the board or Ormandy who wanted to invite Stokowski to guest-conduct.)[15] At his return to the Academy in February 1960, an ecstatic audience rose to greet the 78-year-old conductor, who turned to them with these words: "As I was saying 19 years ago . . ." Laughter answered this typical Stokowski touch. In 1960, 36 of his players were still in the Orchestra. Of course he arranged the Orchestra in his own way, with the strings behind the other instruments. One may wonder how Ormandy really felt about the adulation that Stokowski provoked, but he did write to him personally to invite him for future guest-conducting appearances.

In spite of his unique relationship with the Philadelphia Orchestra, Ormandy accepted some personal engagements away from his Orchestra. In Europe these usually took place in the summer months before the 52-week contract of 1963. As guest conductor of the famous Vienna Philharmonic, he programmed Mahler's music, which the Vienna audience had heard conducted by Mahler himself, by Bruno Walter, and by Richard Strauss. Ormandy was once again taking a huge risk. He had an instinctive understanding of the essence of Mahler's work, which he did not conduct in a literal sense – that is, with rhythms of absolute exactness. Contrary to expectations,

Eugene Ormandy and Leopold Stokowski. Courtesy of the University of
Pennsylvania Rare Book and Manuscript Library

the Viennese audience approved highly of his performance. In Linz, at the Bruckner festival, he substituted, with
almost no rehearsal time, for Bruno Walter, who was ill;
and he conducted without a score. It was another triumph.

During World War II, Ormandy was invited to guest-
conduct in Australia. Under the auspices of the U.S. Office
of War Information, he conducted several concerts organ-
ized for Allied troops. These were pick-up orchestras, but
he received praise for the beauty of the performances.

After his return from Australia, Toscanini invited him
to guest-conduct the NBC Orchestra (June 1944).
In 1947 he conducted President Truman's daughter,
Margaret, in her concert in the Hollywood Bowl, and he
also led the Hollywood Bowl Orchestra in a separate concert that was enthusiastically received. In the Bowl he
conducted his first opera, Puccini's *Madama Butterfly*. Late
in 1950 he made another rare appearance as an opera conductor with his conducting debut at the Metropolitan
Opera in New York in a production of Johann Strauss's
Die Fledermaus.

Ormandy and Rubinstein appeared in late 1947 in
Night Song, an RKO movie about a blind musician who has
composed a concerto. (Merle Oberon, Ethel Barrymore,
and Dana Andrews were the actors in this forgettable
film.) The *New York Times* critic wrote: "If Mr. Rubinstein
and Mr. Ormandy can swallow it [the composition] along

with their pride, they must have pretty strong stomachs."[16] Ormandy did not appear again in the movies.

In November 1959, in the midst of the Cold War, four Soviet musicians shared a concert with the Philadelphia Orchestra. Ormandy programmed the first half with works by the American composers Roger Sessions and Henry Cowell and the second half with a work by each of the three Russian composers present: Dmitri Shostakovich, Dmitri Kabalevsky, and Tikhon Khrennikov. A new cello concerto by Shostakovich was played by the fourth Russian, Mstislav Rostropovich. Van Cliburn, who had won the Tchaikovsky competition in Moscow a year earlier, was in the audience. It was an exciting day that proved the power of music to prevail even in difficult circumstances.

Always cognizant of the impact of the media, Ormandy made frequent use of radio and television. There was a special rivalry between NBC and CBS, and between Ormandy and Toscanini, to present the first television program by a symphony orchestra. NBC announced that Toscanini would conduct the NBC Symphony in an all-Wagner concert on Saturday, March 20, 1948, from 6:30 to 7:30 P.M. CBS immediately announced that Ormandy and the Philadelphia Orchestra would appear at 5:00 P.M., an hour and a half earlier. Thus the Philadelphia Orchestra could claim that its performance was the first major symphony to be televised. Undoubtedly the NBC program was more professional in its technical aspects, but Ormandy's program was somewhat more interesting musically, since the Orchestra played Rachmaninoff's Symphony No. 1 in D Minor, Op. 13, written in 1897 and heard only once before, in St. Petersburg.

Ormandy liked to record and was a fast study when it came to adjusting the sound of the Orchestra to fit the medium. His sense of timing, the speed of his responses, and his ability to work with the sound engineers combined to produce many recordings that, at that period, were unrivaled by other orchestras. Ormandy was a practical musician, always looking out for the financial health of the Orchestra, and he was not averse to making recordings that would sell easily. Nearly four hundred long-playing records, of varying quality, were released during his years with the Orchestra. Most have been converted to compact discs. Three of his recordings were best-selling Gold Records, and his *Catulli Carmina*, by Carl Orff, received a Grammy in 1967. Unlike other music directors, Ormandy only recorded with his own Philadelphia Orchestra.

Recordings for the RCA label provided substantial income for the Orchestra. This source was curtailed, however, when the Federation of Musicians, with James Petrillo as union president, began to object to the loss of revenue caused by jukeboxes and the radio. Although these concerns principally affected popular music, the union succeeded in placing an absolute ban on all recording from 1942 to 1944. Consequently the Philadelphia Orchestra suffered a deficit in the 1943-44 season. In 1943, anticipating the end of the recording ban, the Orchestra changed to the Columbia label for a more advantageous contract that lasted for 25 years. The Philadelphia Orchestra, under Ormandy, became the mainstay of Columbia recordings, and the "Philadelphia sound" came to be recognized internationally. In 1968 the Orchestra returned to RCA, which added a series of much lighter music under the name of the Philadelphia Pops. Columbia feverishly recorded the Orchestra during the last weeks of their contract, and RCA began its recording sessions immediately upon the termination of the Columbia contract. Thus both companies flooded the market with recordings at the same time, with profitable results for the Philadelphia Orchestra.

In spite of the fact that a large percentage of the Orchestra's income came from recordings, there were drawbacks in the recording practices. The musicians complained that the process emphasized economic rather than artistic values. They were sometimes rebuked for an error that necessitated the expense of retaping, when the same error would be overlooked in a concert. Conversely, sometimes Ormandy would let things slide so as to record more in the time allotted. Principal players with solos that would become permanent on records resented being given only one opportunity to record. Occasionally, if there should be unexpected time left at the end of a session, the Orchestra might record something that had not even been rehearsed. Recording practices also disturbed the relationship between music director and players. It rankled that Ormandy received a personal royalty on the sales, while the musicians received an hourly payment.[17]

Strikes plagued the Orchestra, and often these labor disputes were not settled until the season was about to begin, sometimes giving the musicians only one day's rehearsal. In 1954 the first concert was four days late. In 1961 the strike lasted 20 days. The strike in 1966 continued for 58 days, and 35 concerts had to be canceled.[18] Ormandy went to Europe during this period, ostensibly to fulfill previously contracted guest-conducting engagements. He said that he had been asked to stay out of the dispute. Obviously there was bitter criticism of his absence. On the other hand, if he had stayed to be with the musicians, he would have received equal criticism from the opposing side. (Stokowski joined the musicians for a benefit concert in Convention Hall, where he received the usual tumultuous applause.)

A strange antithesis to Ormandy's authoritative approach was the increasing chaos of his closed rehearsals, particularly in his last years, when the musicians talked among themselves and even got up from their chairs and walked around. At one point there were complaints about the disorder, and so the musicians tried a rehearsal with complete attention on the music. Apparently the silence bothered Ormandy, who quipped, "Has someone died?" Astonishing results, however, came from these rehearsals, perhaps because, after so many years, the musicians knew exactly what he wanted from them. In a way, the insecurity that the rehearsals produced, coupled with the vagueness of the conducting signals, meant that the Orchestra, on occasion, functioned somewhat like a chamber group, whose members have to listen to and depend on each other.

As part of their lack of empathy with Ormandy, a few Orchestra players collected "Ormandyisms" that allowed them to poke fun at him surreptitiously. They would take down his sayings during rehearsals under the guise of making important notes on the music. Such jumbled ideas as "It is not together, but the ensemble is perfect," "The notes are right, but if I listened they would be wrong," and "Don't ever follow me because I am difficult," tumbled out constantly in his instructions to the Orchestra. Perhaps this was because of a collision between his fast-paced way of going through rehearsals and his English syntax. These odd expressions, which greatly entertained those who were not fond of Ormandy, are still circulating in the music world.

Although amusing, these sayings do not obscure the fact that Ormandy was very intelligent. It is said that he could figure anybody out as soon as that person entered the room. A consummate politician, he owed his long tenure of 44 years[19] in large part to his shrewdness in surviving the politics that go with being a music director.

Late in 1946 Ormandy again pulled a muscle in his right shoulder, which forced him to withdraw from several concerts. In good spirits, he told the reporters that this had happened three times, and always during the conducting of Tchaikovsky's Fifth Symphony. For most of his life Ormandy suffered from a chronic hip condition (epiphysitis), which produced a slight limp. A serious three-car accident in December 1960, in which he was knocked unconscious for half an hour and suffered deep cuts, aggravated the problem. A hip replacement when he was in his seventies alleviated some of the pain, but his limp became very noticeable.

Ormandy was married twice. In 1922 he married Stephanie Goldner, a harpist whom he met in the Capitol Theater Orchestra. (Later she played in the New York Philharmonic.) Both of their children died shortly after birth of complications from the Rh factor. The marriage ended in divorce in 1947. In 1950 Ormandy married

Margaret Frances Hitsch (Gretel), originally from Vienna, who had become an American citizen and had served with the U.S. Navy during World War II. She was a great asset to him and graciously shared his dedication to Philadelphia. They made their home in the Barclay on Rittenhouse Square.

Ormandy had become an American citizen six years after his arrival in New York. When guest conductor Zoltán Kodály, Ormandy's former composition teacher at the Royal Academy, asked, "Jenö, when are you coming home?" Ormandy is said to have replied, "I am home."[20] It is well known that Ormandy did not like to talk about his early life, and he was very reluctant to discuss his years in the Capitol Theater Orchestra. (Old records of his violin playing show him to be a competent violinist, but probably not of the stature of a concert violinist.)

Ormandy had many sides to his character. He could be severe and stern, even sarcastic. He seemed to enjoy pitting one person against another. He could be supportive and nurturing of young musicians, or he could walk all over them. He had a good sense of humor. Reports say that if any musician sought help from him, he never failed to respond – but not many asked. He was genuinely concerned about the health of his musicians and often was instrumental in obtaining the best doctors for them. He sent flowers when their family members were in the hospital and gave gifts to their young children. He helped Orchestra members to obtain better instruments. He was gracious in remembering personal dates of friends and acquaintances and in thanking people for small favors. However, loyalty to him and to the Orchestra was essential. Increasingly short-tempered in his last years, it became more and more difficult to work with him. Even so, he could be affable and outgoing if he wished, especially, friends said, when Gretel was at his side.[21]

In keeping with the distinctive environment of the Philadelphia Orchestra, the musicians always called him "Mr. Ormandy," never "Eugene." (The custom of using "Maestro" began with Muti.) In spite of the sometimes tenuous relationship between conductor and players, there was enough camaraderie after 23 years so that on Ormandy's sixtieth birthday, when he signaled for the Orchestra to begin Beethoven's *Prometheus* Overture, Op. 28, the Orchestra played "Happy Birthday," and the audience sang along. This good will, however, gradually crumbled as the years went on. Principal players, who were given a certain freedom of expression, were less critical. But in general the musicians grew restive and wanted a fresh approach after such a long regime.

Sadly, as Ormandy reached his eighties, he sometimes became disoriented in his conducting. He continued to lead without a score in front of him, and his increasingly circular manner of conducting masked his confusion from the audience, if not from the musicians. He retired in 1980, very unwillingly, because he wanted to continue in his post as music director. There were no gala celebrations to mark the end of his unusually long directorship because he himself insisted that he was just cutting down on his conducting schedule. He was given the title of conductor laureate, and in this capacity he continued to conduct, although with frequent cancellations. It was clear that he was past his prime. His health began to deteriorate very noticeably in 1983 and 1984. His final performance at Carnegie Hall, on January 10, 1984, included Beethoven's *Leonore* Overture No. 1, Op. 72, and his Symphony No. 6 in F Major, Op. 68 (the *Pastoral*), plus Bartók's Concerto for Orchestra. During the intermission, a stagehand put the Bartók score on the conductor's stand. Ormandy slowly limped to the podium, saw the score, and furiously slammed it shut. He then conducted a flawless Bartók, even proceeding effectively through a rhythmically complex passage that had eluded him in recent past performances. This was, in a way, a triumphant close to his long career.

A few weeks later he suffered a heart attack but recovered. He died of pneumonia on March 12, 1985, at the age of 86. Although his heritage was Jewish, at his wife's request he was buried in the Old Pine Street Churchyard, Pine and Fourth Street, in his beloved Philadelphia.[22]

Through the years, many honors were heaped on Ormandy. He received honorary degrees from the University of Pennsylvania, from the Curtis Institute of Music, from Temple University, and from Rutgers University. Boston University gave him its Citation for Distinguished Service to Music. He received the National Music Council Award of Honor for services to American Music (for American premieres) in 1948. In 1968 he received the Pennsylvania Distinguished Arts Award.

A long list of honors from foreign countries includes the Order of Merit of Juan Pablo Duarte from the Dominican Republic (1945); Officer (1952) and Commander of the French Legion of Honor (1958); Knight of the Order of Dannebrog, first class (1952) and Knight of the Order of the White Rose, Finland (1955); the Sibelius Medal, Finland (1965); the Honor Cross for Arts and Sciences, Austria (1966); and the Golden Medallion of the Vienna Philharmonic (1967); he was designated Commendatore by the Italian government in 1972. During the celebration of the American bicentennial, he was named honorary Knight Commander of the Order of the British Empire (1976).

He received the Philadelphia Award (1970), the National Freedom Award of the Freedoms Foundation (1970), and the Gold Medal of the Union League in Philadelphia (1974). On January 24, 1970, to celebrate

Ormandy's seventieth birthday, President Nixon, on the stage of the Academy of Music, bestowed on him the Freedom Medal, the country's highest civilian award. (Subsequently, the president invited Ormandy and the Orchestra to participate in his second inauguration in January 1973.) In 1982 Ormandy was one of five recipients of the Kennedy Center Honors Awards, and for that occasion he conducted the National Symphony Orchestra in Rachmaninoff's Symphony No. 2 in E Minor, Op. 27.

Although Ormandy brought great honor and prestige to Philadelphia through its famous Orchestra, no city memorials are named for him! Two distinct Ormandy-Stokowski postage stamps were issued. The Philadelphia Orchestra has played many concerts in his honor. A rather shabby reception room in the Academy of Music, called the Ormandy Room, finally underwent extensive renovation in 2004. A colorless banquet hall across the street in the Double Tree Hotel is known as the Ormandy Room. Gretel Ormandy presented her husband's papers, scores, programs, and recordings to the University of Pennsylvania, and there is a Eugene Ormandy Center in the Otto Albrecht Music Library. In 1999, on the hundredth anniversary of Ormandy's birth, the collection formed part of a University of Pennsylvania Library exhibition.

The Philadelphia Orchestra is always acclaimed as one of the greatest orchestras in the world, yet a small sprinkling of critics[23] have denied Ormandy equal stature. A gray area of dispute centers on the depth and imagination of his interpretations. He has been accused of little variation in style, to the point that Haydn, Mozart, Brahms, and Tchaikovsky are consistently touched with much the same lush sound. In his emphasis on sound, he tended to stress brilliant, exterior effects and to work in large layers rather than in small subtleties. All this contributed to a perception, in some circles, of superficiality.

Ormandy did not have a strong foundation of musical philosophy to rely on in his conducting. Rather, he was an intuitive musician and an intuitive conductor. He was never restricted by a literal rendition of the music. Thus he has provoked great admiration as well as disparagement.

A fair assessment of Ormandy should take into account that he was a serious, dedicated music director who conscientiously brought twentieth-century works into his concerts, unearthed worthwhile music that had been forgotten or ignored, and conducted an astonishing number of world and U.S. premieres. He has never been given sufficient credit for these efforts, perhaps because he was always associated with music from the Romantic era. The verdict is unanimous that he was magnificent in conducting the orchestral accompaniment of soloists, who clamored to perform with him. He was unsurpassed at producing beautiful sound that delighted audiences.

Above all was his absolute devotion and dedication to the Philadelphia Orchestra.

Many of the members of his Orchestra grew tired of him after so many years, and for a long time their known frustrations colored his reputation. Fortunately, with the filter of time, Ormandy's extraordinary musical gifts are being acknowledged with increasing appreciation and respect.[24]

(previous) Riccardo Muti in rehearsal. Adrian Siegel Collection, courtesy of the Philadelphia Orchestra Association Archives

ᒑᑫ Riccardo Muti ᒋᑐ

The choice of Ormandy's successor became a topic of speculation, rumor, and gossip in Philadelphia and in the music world beyond. As early as 1968, Ormandy was asked in an interview with Herbert Kupferberg if he had considered what kind of successor he would like to see. After assuring the questioner that he was not ready to retire, Ormandy gave his candid description of the conductor who, in his opinion, should lead the Philadelphia Orchestra in the future: "The conductor who comes here should be an outstanding, well-rounded musician, even if he's only thirty years old. . . . He should be able to present a variety of programs—classics, romantics, contemporaries. He should be prepared to stay—I don't think the board of directors would engage a man, even today, even with the fifty-two week season, who would want to conduct less than half the season. He should be willing to become a leader in the community. All of that combined would make the kind of conductor who should take over the Philadelphia Orchestra."[1]

In a way, Ormandy was expressing the lingering hope of many that a conductor could be found who would give his principal loyalty to one orchestra—in the mold of Ormandy himself. But the mobility of the jet age, the lure of lucrative contracts, and the prestige of competing for guest-conductor appearances had already won. Ormandy must have understood the impossibility of his ideal, since he considered Riccardo Muti "his" discovery, and Muti certainly did not give any evidence of wishing to be anchored to one place and one orchestra. It was Ormandy's ability to recognize real talent that overrode any other consideration.

Muti first encountered Ormandy in Florence in May 1970 during one of the Philadelphia Orchestra's European tours. The Orchestra had scheduled a rehearsal in the Teatro Comunale in Florence in order to become familiar with the acoustics of the theater. Ormandy and some of the Orchestra staff arrived early, during another rehearsal, with Muti on the podium. The young, dynamic conductor so impressed Ormandy that he invited Muti, with others, to a private luncheon. And Muti was engaged as a guest conductor in Philadelphia for the fall of 1972.

Muti's background and musical education were typically Italian. He was born in Naples on July 28, 1941, but his childhood was spent in the southern province of Apulia. It was a quiet family life, with no sports and no

Riccardo Muti and Eugene Ormandy. Courtesy of the University of Pennsylvania Rare Book and Manuscript Library

television. His father was a physician who loved music, and each of his five sons played an instrument. Riccardo began violin lessons at age eight, but switched to the piano at 12. Eventually the family moved back to Naples, principally for better educational opportunities.

Muti entered the Conservatorio di Música San Pietro a Majella at age 17, with plans for a career as a pianist. Steeped in tradition, the Conservatorio proudly proclaimed that Donizetti had been the director and that Bellini had studied there. At one point Muti was recruited to take over the direction of a student orchestra and rehearse a Bach concerto with them on the next day. When he raised his baton and heard his ideas coming forth in the music, he knew that he wanted to be a conductor. He often repeated that it was a wonderful moment of discovery that everyone should experience in some way. While preparing for his piano finals, he enrolled at the University of Naples, where he studied philosophy for three semesters. After he received his diploma from the Conservatorio, he continued his education at the Giuseppe Verdi Conservatorio in Milan, studying conducting with Antonino Votto, a former assistant to Toscanini, and composition with Bruno Bettinelli, who also taught Claudio Abbado. (Muti believes in the necessity of a knowledge of composition. He says that you can conduct without it, but you cannot interpret the music.)

In his second year in Milan, he was the accompanist for one of the Conservatorio's classes in singing. In this class he met a mezzo soprano, María Cristina Mazzavillani, whom he married four years later. He graduated from the Verdi Conservatorio in 1966, with honors and with diplomas in both conducting and composition.

At the time that he met Ormandy, Muti was making a name for himself in Italy and was poised for European recognition. In 1967 he had been the first Italian to win the Guido Cantelli International Competition for Conductors. There is a little-known story about Muti's preparation for this competition. He had caught the attention of a baroness when he was a student at the Verdi Conservatorio. She hired an orchestra in Prague, and for a week Muti rehearsed with them. Then he and the orchestra toured northern Italy for almost two weeks, with his patroness paying all the expenses.[2] While this gave Muti an advantage, it does not negate the conducting ability that he exhibited and that won him the competition.

Later he made his symphonic conducting debut as guest conductor of the Radiotelevisione Italiana (RAI) Orchestra of Milan. One of the judges at the Guido Cantelli competition had been Vittorio Gui, formerly a principal assistant of Toscanini and founder of the Maggio Musicale Fiorentino. When a scheduled conductor fell ill, Gui invited Muti to conduct a concert with Sviatoslav

Richter as the guest soloist. The question arose whether Richter would accept such a fledgling conductor; after rehearsing with Muti, Richter warmly agreed. The performance was to have taken place in March 1968 but was canceled because of a general strike in Florence. This was a fortunate break for Muti, since the concert was held later, during the May Music Festival, which attracted visitors from all over the world.

Muti's professional career as conductor of opera began at the Autunno Musicale Napoletano in October 1969. Outside Italy, Muti's international recognition began with operatic guest-conducting appearances at the Salzburg Festival in 1971, when he was 30, and symphonic guest conducting with the Berlin Philharmonic in 1972.

On October 27, 1972, Muti made his U.S. debut as guest conductor of the Philadelphia Orchestra. The program consisted of Mozart's Symphony No. 34 in C, K 338, and his Piano Concerto No. 9 in E Flat, K 271 (Philippe Entremot, pianist), plus Prokofiev's Symphony No. 3 in C Minor, Op. 44. The young, handsome Italian was an immediate success; the Orchestra itself gave him a standing ovation. On the strength of this achievement, his manager, Ronald Wilford, was able to obtain engagements for him during the next few years with the Boston, Cleveland, and Chicago symphonies. Unfortunately, a scheduled appearance with the New York Philharmonic ran into difficulty because Muti became ill in Italy, and somehow the New York orchestra never received notice of the reason for his failure to arrive.

Muti returned to Philadelphia to guest-conduct every year after his initial performance, and in 1977 he was appointed principal guest conductor of the Philadelphia Orchestra, a post that included two months of conducting every winter season. The title "principal guest conductor" had never been used by the Philadelphia Orchestra, although it was customary in London. It was first used in the United States by the Chicago Symphony in 1969, when the title was given to Carlo María Giulini at the same time that Georg Solti was named music director.

Muti's Italian and international career was in full swing during this period. In Florence, which became his major operatic headquarters, he led two productions a year, one during the Teatro Comunale's winter season, and one for the May Festival, plus one other opera elsewhere. He established a reputation for brilliant performances, particularly of Italian and French opera. Unyielding on the subject of original texts, in 1972 he conducted an uncut *Guillaume Tell* that lasted six hours, from 8:00 P.M. until 2:00 A.M. He guest-conducted at La Scala (1973), the Vienna State Opera (1973), the Bavarian State Opera in Munich, and Covent Garden in London (1977). His orchestral appearances included the Vienna Philharmonic

(1974), yearly performances with the Berlin Philharmonic, and major orchestras in Budapest, Amsterdam,
and Madrid.

Later in the same year in which he first conducted the
Philadelphia Orchestra (1972), he guest-conducted the
New Philharmonia Orchestra in London. Impressed by
his energy and decisiveness, the orchestra members asked
him to become the principal conductor (1973) and, six
years later, to be the music director (1979). This was an
orchestra in disarray that was trying to find a successor
to the ailing 86-year-old Otto Klemperer. The musicians
were disheartened, and their playing was listless and
ragged. Muti brought a breath of fresh air and vitality to
the orchestra. He added young players; he enhanced the
program offerings; he formed them into a precise ensemble. The financial situation also improved under Muti. In
1964 the orchestra had been abandoned by EMI and was
able to survive only through the efforts of Klemperer and
Giulini. At that point it had changed its original name of
Philharmonia to the New Philharmonia. As Klemperer
grew older and Giulini's career took him elsewhere, the
orchestra continued to decline. With the arrival of this
new charismatic conductor, however, EMI renewed its
contract with the orchestra and Muti, principally to record
opera. In 1977 the orchestra went back to its original
name. By the time Muti's rival, Claudio Abbado, joined

the London Symphony Orchestra, they had to contend with an invigorated, thriving Philharmonia.

In Italy the mercurial Muti had been known for his stubbornness and for being a hothead. During his first appearance in La Scala (1973), he had furiously thrown down his baton and walked out, exasperated by the leading singer's refusal to pay attention to his directions. He then boycotted that opera house for more than ten years. In Florence, because of the incompetence of the artistic director, Muti was responsible for organizing a strike that involved the orchestra, chorus, and ballet, and that continued for three months until the director was fired. But in England he was much quieter and friendlier to the musicians, while maintaining a certain aloofness.

In Philadelphia, during Ormandy's last years, various conductors were being considered for the position of music director, but no one satisfied Ormandy or the board, and a few names were unacceptable to the musicians. Although Muti's conducting style contrasted sharply with Ormandy's, his appointment as permanent guest conductor had had Ormandy's approval. In a way, it served as a kind of apprenticeship, somewhat like Ormandy's with Stokowski. It was obvious that Muti was the likely candidate for the music directorship.

In the 1979-80 season, Ormandy finally announced that this would be his last as music director. In May the appointment of Riccardo Muti as music director was announced officially,[3] to begin in the 1980-81 season. Muti would conduct for 10 weeks in his first season of 39 concerts; there would be 55 appearances in 14 weeks in 1981-82, and 60 concerts in 15 weeks in the last year of a three-year contract. In a 1978 interview with Daniel Webster of the *Philadelphia Inquirer*,[4] Muti said he had told the trustees that he could not settle in and just conduct the Orchestra, that it was necessary for him, and for the good of the Orchestra, that he conduct opera and work in different settings. At the time of his appointment, he continued his operatic commitments in Florence and remained as music director of the Philharmonia Orchestra in London, but he relinquished both posts in 1982. He continued, however, to guest-conduct with top European orchestras, and in 1986 he became the principal conductor of La Scala.

Muti's impact on the Philadelphia Orchestra was immediate. He expected a disciplined ensemble and strict adherence to what was written in the score. He did not feel that the Orchestra measured up to his standards; in fact, he was appalled at the laxity of attacks and the occasional faulty intonations. His conducting technique elicited a simultaneous beginning attack with absolute rhythmic precision—quite different from the expansive, elongated rhythm to which the Orchestra was accustomed. He was not so much interested in the sound in the Academy of Music – and never once did he go out into the hall to judge the sound – as he was in balance and proportion and clarity. What he wanted was a clean sound more in line with what record companies demanded, and he did not want one instrumental section to dominate the others. The Orchestra, he felt, should be in accord with present-day practices. His approach, after Ormandy, was revolutionary. Yet Muti objected to any comparisons with Ormandy's style. He made it clear that the dissimilarities resulted from differences in personality as well as ideas of interpretation. Muti always treated Ormandy with great respect, and he said that they were friends.

Even before he became the music director, Muti had had his doubts about the meaning of the "Philadelphia sound." He asked, "It's a publicity thing, isn't it?"[5] Generally, under his baton, the Orchestra's tone became lighter and more balanced. This different tonal quality was not as noticeable in recordings, where the engineers can make alterations almost at will; but in concert the difference was easy to recognize. Those who had loved the Orchestra's distinctive massive sheen of sound complained that Muti was making the Philadelphia Orchestra indistinguishable from any other symphony orchestra. His answer was that he wanted a different sound for every composer rather than a consistent lushness for every style.

Replacing a successful director after so many years is not an easy task. Inevitably the orchestra becomes accustomed to play standard works in one way, and it was a challenge to Muti to supplant deeply engraved concepts. Fortunately for him, the musicians were very pleased with his conducting and felt that he was warm and approachable, within limits. Many thought that he had the best baton technique that they had ever worked with, and they found it especially easy to respond to his vertical, precise conducting. He often sang passages to illustrate how he wanted them to be played. To him the players were not subordinates, and he corrected errors with politeness as well as with authority.

Muti's magnetism and good looks appealed to the audience. He crossed the stage rapidly, lean body erect and graceful like a young *torero*. His mane of black hair, luminous dark eyes, patrician nose, and sensual mouth all contributed to his glamorous podium personality. The newspapers wrote about a new matinee idol. In addition, he conducted with an intensity that was felt by the audience, and with dramatic gestures that were fascinating to watch. His performances always generated excitement. Muti was aware of his effect on the audience, and he frequently spoke against the "cult of the conductor." He cautioned that a conductor should not draw too much attention to himself while on the podium because this might negate the audience's appreciation of the music. Those who have played under his baton feel that his dramatic gestures are genuine, not put on for show.

He was almost fanatical about playing the original and uncut version of a composition. When he recorded Beethoven's Symphony No. 7 in A, Op. 92, he insisted upon taking all the repeats, which added 12 minutes, and he continued this practice in conducting Mozart's Symphony No. 41 in C (*Jupiter*), K 551, which also added considerable length to the performance. He felt strongly that no one has the right to tamper with the score as it was written, not even soloists. In one of his early appearances, he surprised the players by correcting their parts of Mozart's Symphony No. 36 in C (*Linz*), K 425, according to a new, critical edition of Bärenreiter, which removed former additions and mistakes. Muti took great pains to illustrate Mozart's phrasing and the style of eighteenth-century string playing. He slimmed down the Orchestra for Mozart, which resulted in a lighter sound and a more authentic interpretation. He also favored little-known works of famous composers. The Orchestra respected his decisions. Once in a while they would complain among themselves about being overworked in rehearsals, but in general they admired Muti's dedication to the music and his scrupulous attention to details.

His insistence on the complete and original score was due in part to his conviction that the public should hear the music exactly as the composer intended. In addition, playing a master's little-known works would, in his opinion, contribute to the audience's deeper understanding of that composer. All this reflected Muti's belief in his mission to educate the public. On one occasion he said, "Music is more than just a pleasure. It's a very potent civilizing force, and like the other Arts, an integral part of a people's education."[6] Nothing infuriated him more in Philadelphia than the concept of music as entertainment, often illustrated by reviews or discussions of symphonic works coupled in the Arts and Entertainment section of the newspaper.

Muti's repertoire was extensive and eclectic. He conducted more Mozart and Beethoven than some conductors of his age group. He played a great deal of Russian music. He programmed concert operas and major choral works. When Muti came to Philadelphia, he admitted that he was unfamiliar with American music but hoped to correct this deficiency. (The story goes that once, when someone pushed a microphone into his face and asked if he was going to play American music, he replied, "Is there any?")[7] The two ASCAP awards of 1987 and 1991, for Muti's and the Orchestra's leading role in championing new American music, illustrate his determination to overcome his lack of knowledge in this area.

From 1972 to 1992, Muti conducted 85 first performances with the Philadelphia Orchestra, from De Angelis'

Suite of Sixteenth-Century Lute Music for Harp and Chamber Orchestra, through well-known composers' works that had not been played before in Philadelphia, to contemporary compositions.

Muti had a special interest in music from the contemporary period, and many musicians in the Orchestra think that, because of his precise stick technique, this is where he was at his best. He expected his audiences to learn to appreciate this music, whether they wanted to or not. It would never have occurred to him to consider the board's economic concerns about scaring away audiences with unfamiliar music, nor the cost of additional rehearsal time to prepare the new music. At the very beginning of his directorship, Muti declared, through the press, that "the Board worked for the Orchestra, not the other way around."[8]

The 85 first performances that he conducted included nine world premieres:

Ezra Laderman, Concerto for Flute, Bassoon and Orchestra, 1982-83
Raymond Premprú, Music for Three Trombones, Tuba, and Orchestra, 1984-85
Richard Wernick, Violin Concerto, 1985-86
Christopher Rouse, *Phaeton*, 1986-87
Ralph Shapey, Symphonic Concertante, 1986-87
Steven Stucky, Concerto for Orchestra, 1988-89

Joseph Castaldo, Viola Concerto, 1989-90
Marcel Farago, *In Memoriam*, 1989-90
Bernard Rands, *Ceremonial 3*, 1990-91

Among Muti's major contributions to the Philadelphia Orchestra programming was his introduction of
concert opera performances. He wanted audiences to
know not only that opera was more than the mere trap-
pings of scenery and costumes, but that in opera the
orchestra was of the utmost importance and required an
ensemble capable of shading and subtleties. In playing
with singers, Muti believes that an orchestra becomes
more flexible and learns to play symphonic music in a different way.

In the 1983-84 season, Verdi's *Macbeth* (U.S. premiere
of a critical edition) became the first concert opera to be
presented, followed by:

Gluck's *Orfeo et Euridice* (original 1762 version),
   1983-84
Verdi's *Rigoletto* (U.S. premiere of a critical edition),
   1985-86
Wagner's *Der fliegende Holländer*, 1986-87
Verdi's *Nabucco* (U.S. premiere of a critical edition),
   1988-89
Puccini's *Tosca*, 1991-92 (recorded)[9]
Leoncavallo's *Pagliacci*, 1991-92 (recorded)

The opera *Pagliacci*, with tenor Luciano Pavarotti, proved to be the audience's favorite in the roster of concert operas. Five of these concert operas were also presented in New York and received enthusiastic praise from critics and audiences alike.

Many in the Orchestra feel that Muti was especially good at working with singers. He was always intensely involved with their performances, and even preferred to take the piano rehearsals himself to foster a better understanding between conductor and performer. He demanded correct enunciation in all languages and insisted that singers understand the meaning of the words. Singers showered praises on Muti, citing especially his understanding of the voice. Always very strict, Muti was particularly adamant about sticking to the composer's text, and sometimes a singer reacted against his removal of an expected high note or expected trills and ornamentation because they were not in the original score. He once told Pavarotti, "Either sing what Bellini wrote or find yourself a new conductor."[10]

Among the singers who have performed with Muti and the Philadelphia Orchestra are Jessye Norman, Plácido Domingo, Mirella Freni, Luciano Pavarotti, Frederica von Stade, Samuel Ramey, José Carreras, and Kathleen Battle. Solo instrumentalists include Claudio Arrau, Pinchas Zuckerman, Maurizio Pollini, Yo-Yo Ma, Yehudi Menuhin,

Radu Lupu, Isaac Stern, Rudolph Serkin, Kyung-Wha Chung, Itzhak Perlman, Murray Perahia, André Watts, and Sarah Chang (at 10 years of age).

His discography is impressive.[11] His recording of Verdi's *Macbeth* brought him the André Messager Prize as "the best conductor of 1977"; his recording of Mendelssohn's Symphony No. 3 in A Minor, Op. 56 (*Scottish*), earned the Deutsche Schaliplatten Preis as "the best symphonic recording of 1977"; his recording of Liszt's *Les Préludes*, 1982-83, won the Gran Prix from the Franz Liszt Society in Budapest. Many other recordings have won international awards, such as his recording of Mahler's Symphony No. 1 in D (1984), which is especially interesting because in the seventies Muti said that he had not yet conducted any Mahler.

With the Philadelphia Orchestra he has 70 recordings, including the complete Beethoven cycle of symphonies. Symphony No. 6 in F, Op. 68 (*Pastoral*), plus Symphony No. 7 in A, Op. 92, was Muti's first recording with the Orchestra, and the entire cycle was the first recorded by an American orchestra for compact disc. Also with the Philadelphia Orchestra he has recorded the complete Brahms symphonies, and the three Scriabin symphonies, the latter a comparatively rare undertaking. A few critics question whether these recordings hold up well today.[12] Muti himself has been skeptical about the significance of recorded music, and he has spoken about the loss of artistic creativity because of a constant preoccupation with the technological aspects of sound. However, in contrast to the recordings made when he was in his forties, Muti's 2004 release of Tchaikovsky's Symphony No. 6 (*Pathetique*), with the Orchestre National de France, shows a much greater depth of interpretation. The advancing years seem to have brought with them more mature concepts.

Muti has received many awards and honors: the Illica-Giacosa Prize in 1971; Grande Ufficiale and Cavalieri de Gran Croce of the Italian Republic; Order of the Cross from the Federal Republic of Germany; the Cross of Honor from Austria; and the Commendatore Cross of the Cavalieri in Malta. He is an Honorary Ambassador to the United Nations High Commissioner for Refugees; an Honorary Member of the Royal Academy of Music (London); and an Honorary Member of the Accademia di Santa Cecilia (Rome) and of the Accademia Luigi Cherubini (Florence). In 1988 he received the Viotti d'Oro from La Scala. In 1991 he was awarded the Ehrenring (Ring of Honor) of the Vienna Philharmonic; and, in 1992, he was named Commander of the French Legion of Honor.

He has honorary doctorates from the University of Pennsylvania, from the Curtis Institute of Music, and from Westminster Choir College, Mount Holyoke College,

Warwick University in England, and the Universities of Bologna, Urbino, and Cremona.

He received the Philadelphia Art Alliance Medal of Achievement and the Pennsylvania Governor's Distinguished Arts Award, 1989.

As conductor of the Orchestra, Muti was responsible for the concept of the work and for the quality of orchestral performances. As music director, he was responsible for all programming and for the selection of soloists and guest conductors. Because of his many outside commitments, a noticeable augmentation of guest conductors began during his leadership. He particularly wanted guest conductors who would complement his repertoire and thus give the public a complete musical experience.

Muti cut out the Orchestra's longstanding appearances in Ann Arbor, in Washington, and in Baltimore. Unlike Stokowski and Ormandy, he did not take the Orchestra to such unlikely spots as Wanamaker's or train platforms. His idea of incorporating the Orchestra into the life of the community concentrated on education of both adults and students. Many of his approaches for reaching new audiences have been continued. He placed emphasis on area students and actively encouraged them to attend rehearsals, although he did not conduct either the Children's or Student Concerts. He established "Opera Week," where he and opera scholars discussed with the public the opera being given that season. Films, slides, lectures, and round-table discussions by critics and musicologists, in collaboration with the University of Pennsylvania, were part of the plan. During "It's Your Orchestra Week" (1985), a great many winners in a drawing were able to attend a free concert in the Academy, conducted by Muti and broadcast live on WIOQ-FM. For those who had never attended an orchestra concert before, he introduced some of the music; visitors were permitted to go backstage after the event. The "Come and Meet the Music" series featured Muti's introductions to the programs, telecast live on KYW-TV3 and on WFLN-FM in 1989 and 1990.

Important telecasts showed off the Orchestra. "The Fabulous Philadelphians: From Ormandy to Muti," a six-part television series co-produced with WHYY-TV, was aired nationwide on PBS in 1981. Berlioz's *"Symphonie Fantastique:* A Conductor's View" was aired nationally on PBS in 1985. Concerts were taped in Tokyo in 1986 and 1989. The 1992 Gala Tribute to Riccardo Muti, with many well-known singers and instrumentalists, was telecast live on KYW-TV and simulcast on WFLN.

The Philadelphia Orchestra Chamber Music series, formerly discouraged, was begun during the Muti era. Musicians from the Orchestra performed in the Academy Ballroom on Sunday afternoons. Muti himself is a good, but not a great, pianist, and he joined the chamber group only once. Outside solo performances by members of the Orchestra became possible. In fact, Muti was known to telephone a soloist after his performance to inquire about the concert.

Illustrating his devotion to all the arts, Muti and the Orchestra led a campaign that raised money for the Philadelphia Ballet. Reflecting his social interests, he conducted three "Concerts for Humanity," in 1983, 1984, and 1988, to benefit organizations dedicated to halting the nuclear arms buildup.

Muti usually rehearsed once a year with the student orchestra of the Curtis Institute of Music. Although he said that he regretted the lack of tradition in American institutes of music – the kind of tradition that was the basis of his Italian musical education – he applauded the fact that Curtis students have more opportunities for contact with performing artists and conductors.

More than most conductors, Muti was extremely sensitive to extraneous noises: coughing, rattling of programs, clapping incorrectly between movements, whispering, or talking. He often glared at the audience for these offenses, and once, when he was on the podium and ready to conduct, he turned to the audience with ferocity and demanded that they keep still. Those who arrived late had to wait to be seated until the first composition was finished, an edict that angered some longtime subscribers.

Muti has his own method of preparing a new score. As in everything else, he takes an intellectual approach. First he examines the music from a historical as well as an artistic viewpoint. Then he studies the score itself. Next he takes it to the piano and plays it through. And then, away from the piano, he begins an in-depth analysis. When he feels that he has the structure and the sound in his mind, he returns to the piano and plays the entire score. He needs, of course, to "hear" mentally the ensemble of the various instruments. He uses recordings only when he wants to hear something special from a conductor of the past–Toscanini, Bruno Walter, Wilhelm Furtwangler, all before his time. He does not conduct from memory as Ormandy did, and also Sawallisch on many occasions. Muti's forte is to prepare carefully and conscientiously, even for some contemporary work that he will never conduct again.

Muti toured with the Philadelphia Orchestra in the United States, the Far East, Europe, and South America. His first tour, together with Ormandy, was a 1980 trip through the United States and Asia. In his European tour of 1983–84, he made his first appearance with the Orchestra in his native Italy, visiting Naples and La Scala in Milan. The 1984–85 tour of the Far East included the Orchestra's first appearance in Hong Kong. Having conducted annually in the Salzburg Festival for more than twenty years, Muti took the Philadelphia Orchestra there for its debut in 1987. The same tour included a second appearance in La Scala and a television broadcast in Frankfurt. In the 1990–91 season, the European tour included the Orchestra's first appearance in Prague and Bologna, plus returns to Florence and Milan. The 1991–92 tour was Muti's last with the Philadelphia Orchestra, with performances in Seville, Barcelona, Madrid, Ravenna, Genoa, Vienna, London, Brussels, and the first concerts in Tel Aviv and Jerusalem.

In 1986, when Muti became the principal conductor of La Scala, and then its music director, he was adding a second major post to his responsibilities as music director of the Philadelphia Orchestra. His archenemy, Claudio Abbado, had been the principal conductor of the orchestra at La Scala (1968) and the music director for 14 years until he left in 1986. The Abbados were key figures in Milan; Abbado's uncle had been the head of the Verdi Conservatorio, and his father, a violinist, had been on the faculty. The enmity between Abbado and Muti was well known, although its origin has never been disclosed by either one. Perhaps it has something to do with the subtle prejudices between northern and southern Italy. Muti was accustomed to criticize Abbado in public but toned down his derision when he got to La Scala. He used the term "predecessor" if it was necessary, but never spoke

Abbado's name. Certain conductors who had flocked to guest-conduct at La Scala when Abbado held the reins later avoided appearing there. You were either in the Abbado camp or in the Muti camp.

After Abbado left La Scala, Muti initially rejected the management's attempts to interest him in coming to Milan. He did, however, respond to an appeal by the musicians. His arrival on the scene was electrifying. As always when he took over an orchestra or an opera house, he brought his own ideas and interpretations instead of following what had been the norm. He began to gather a team of young musicians around him as Toscanini had done. He brought back Wagner operas and ignored the tradition of inviting only northern Europeans to conduct them. He presented a wide range of productions, including little-known and seldom performed operas. He insisted upon authenticity. He announced, "Here we will avoid the cheap things that are heard in some opera houses where singers or conductors have no respect for the text."[13] His artistic policies, of course, provoked controversy. Nevertheless, there is general agreement that Muti was very successful in energizing the performances as well as improving the orchestra and stabilizing La Scala's finances. His La Scala enjoyed great prestige.

Muti never really adapted to living in Philadelphia. When his children were young, his wife, Cristina, remained in Italy except for special concerts or events. This meant that during most of his weeks of conducting the Orchestra, he lived alone in the Academy House, an apartment building adjacent to the Academy of Music. When the children were older, Cristina was able to accompany him somewhat more often. On tours of the United States, he often complained about the food, and in general he was not impressed with life in America, nor did he fit into the American scene. In spite of the many later tributes, he disliked having to socialize and cozy up to wealthy patrons. In Italy he derided the provincialism that he found in Philadelphia, and there are reports that some of his remarks found their way into Italian newspapers.

Essentially Muti is a family man, which contrasts with his cosmopolitan life. Any free time that he has is spent with his wife and their three children (a daughter and two sons). Their home is in Ravenna, a three-hour trip from Milan, which Muti drives with breakneck speed. They live in a 400-year-old house, modernized and filled with books, scores, records, and souvenirs of his career. He can roam around Ravenna, often on his bicycle, and the local people sometimes stop him and comment on a musical event.[14] Cristina gave up any idea of having her own singing career when they were married. Muti says that she is a well-rounded musician, and he considers her his best critic.

Muti always worried openly about being absent from his children so much of the time, and he hoped that they knew they were as essential to him as his music. Neither parent was anxious for the children to be musicians—unless that is what they really wanted. The children are grown now, and have entered other professions: law, architecture, and acting.

Early in his appointment as music director of the Philadelphia Orchestra, Muti began agitating for a new symphony hall. The Academy of Music, with its dry acoustics and incessant subway rumblings, plus its tendency to obscure subtleties, was not suitable for the precision and clarity that Muti sought. He pointed to the contrasting splendor of sound when the Orchestra played in Carnegie Hall. To record, the Orchestra was forced to use the broken-down Metropolitan Opera House on North Broad Street, sometimes in winter with the snow falling on the musicians while they played; or the gymnasium of Memorial Hall in Fairmont Park, where the loud heating system needed to be turned off during the recording session, leaving the musicians to shiver in the cold. For a while it seemed that Muti's efforts to bring about a new hall were going to succeed. A model of the proposed new building stood in the entrance of the Academy, and it appeared that it might be possible to raise adequate money. Unfortunately there was not sufficient support from either the private sector or the government, and, citing various objections, neither the Annenberg nor the Pew foundations would contribute. Muti became entangled in the squabbles over the proposed $100 million hall, and when money from Annenberg was directed, instead, for renovations to the Academy – particularly the sums to be spent on new bathrooms on the ground floor – his ire was openly expressed. The collapse of the original plans infuriated him.

When Herbert von Karajan died on July 16, 1989, the race was on for a new music director for the famed Berlin Philharmonic. The three foremost contenders were Loren Maazel, James Levine, and Riccardo Muti. Muti had reason to believe that he was favorably positioned. Karajan had invited him to guest-conduct every season since his first appearance in 1972; he had recorded with the Berlin Philharmonic; he was well accepted in Salzburg and in Vienna; he had a splendid reputation as music director of the Philadelphia Orchestra; he was secure at La Scala. But it was Claudio Abbado who was victorious! Muti, apparently, was deeply shaken. With his enemy in power, his hopes for a permanent appointment in Berlin were dashed.

Abruptly, he tendered his resignation as music director of the Philadelphia Orchestra in March 1990. In an emotional press conference, he spoke of the pressure and stress that he had been under and the necessity for rest and for a "real life." He burst out with the statement, "Now no one will be able to say that I want this hall built for me."[15] His announcement was greeted with shock by the board, and with regret and dismay by most of the Orchestra members and the public.

The reasons for Muti's unexpected decision to leave are open to speculation. Many think he could not accept the failure of the plans for a new concert hall, in addition to the strained relations between the board and himself. Others believe that his ultimate goal had always been the music directorship of the very prestigious Berlin Philharmonic (which would have allowed him to live in Europe as opposed to the United States). Did he think of the Philadelphia Orchestra as a stepping stone to his goal? Opera was surely his deepest love. Was his position at La Scala sufficient for him? Some simply accept him at his word: he was homesick for a life with his family in his own country. Probably there is a kernel of truth in all these reasons.

Muti agreed to continue until the end of the 1991–92 season, at which time he would become conductor laureate. A gala concert on April 22, 1992, celebrated his years in Philadelphia. The televised program featured works by Verdi, Mozart, George Rochberg, Bernard Rands, Puccini, Martucci, Peter Christian Lutkin, Dvořák, and Ravel, with soloists Samuel Ramey, bass; Frederica von Stade, mezzo soprano; Carol Vanessa, soprano; Luciano

Pavarotti, tenor; Kyung-Wha Chung, violin; Gidon Kremer, violin; and the Westminster Symphonic Choir. Letters in a gala book never express negativity, but, even so, in *Riccardo Muti: Twenty Years in Philadelphia*, the expressions of admiration, loyalty, and regret at his leaving ring with warmth and sincerity.[16] The picture of Muti as a good friend, thoughtful, empathetic, tirelessly devoted to his post as music director, contrasts sharply with the opposite view of Muti as a loner, aloof, arrogant, scornful of Philadelphia's provincialism.

Anticipation of Muti's frequent returns to Philadelphia as conductor laureate touched every tribute. But this did not happen as expected. He returned for two subscription concerts only, February 5 and February 6, 1993; five years later, he appeared for the Musicians' Pension Fund Concert, October 5, 1998; and he returned again for the Pension Fund Concert of February 13, 2005. In contrast, he made his debut with the New York Philharmonic in 1999 and appeared 15 times with that orchestra up to 2002, in addition to several performances in 2004 and 2005. These frequent guest-conducting performances with the New York Philharmonic are considered snubs that register deeply in Philadelphia. Many of the Philadelphia Orchestra members felt hurt and even betrayed. In a review of Wolfgang Sawallisch's first return as conductor laureate, some 12 years later, resentment toward Muti can still be felt: "And that a former Music Director of the orchestra [Sawallisch] is fulfilling his duties as Conductor Laureate at all is a nice thing, since Riccardo Muti seems much happier toiling away in New York, Vienna, and Milan."[17]

Quietly, Muti's title of conductor laureate disappeared from the Orchestra's letterhead and from programs and official announcements. On July 18, 2000, Muti rejected an offer to become music director of the New York Philharmonic. He announced his decision personally to several music critics, to the relief of some in both New York and Philadelphia, although for different reasons.

Since leaving Philadelphia, Muti has devoted much of his energy to opera productions of La Scala. His European guest appearances beyond La Scala have been mainly with the Vienna Philharmonic, and he no longer appears regularly at the Salzburg Festival nor with the Berlin Philharmonic. In July 2001, Muti turned 60, a point at which greatness should have been realized, or at least hover on the threshold. He has achieved international stature, but whether he stands permanently among the great conductors has not been decided. In 2001, David Patrick Stearns, music critic of the *Philadelphia Inquirer*, described Muti as having hit the proverbial glass ceiling, an assessment that he also applied to Ormandy. "They reached a point in their artistic lives when they began to apply the same technique (rhythmic muscle, lush sound) to almost every piece before them."[18]

Muti clearly turned his back on the Philadelphia Orchestra. More than once he was invited to return to guest-conduct, but he always declined, presumably because of his heavy conducting schedule. His return in 2005 for the Musicians' Pension Fund Concert, therefore, was a surprising reversal.

During the difficult contract negotiations in the fall of 2004, the musicians themselves suggested a benefit concert to help allay the effects of budget cuts, and they contacted Muti directly. The result mirrors Muti's earlier reaction to requests from Milan: his initial rejection of the efforts by La Scala's management to persuade him to come there, followed by a positive response to an appeal by the musicians. Muti and all the musicians involved donated their performance fees for the concert on February 13, 2005.

It was Muti's first experience in Verizon Hall. Amid all the discussion about acoustical problems, Muti called the acoustics "fantastic" and "wonderful." With unabashed affection he greeted the players who had been in the Orchestra during his years as music director, and he made the acquaintance of the many players who were engaged by Sawallisch during his decade-long tenure – actually one-third of the Orchestra.

Muti conducting at the February 13, 2005, Musicians' Pension Fund Concert.
Reprinted by permission of The Philadelphia Inquirer/John Costello

Muti, at 63, looked much older than the dashing figure that everyone remembered, but the excitement associated with his podium personality remained the same. In
addition to the expected electricity in his conducting, there
was evidence of an increasing maturity of interpretation.
In assessing his Brahms Symphony No. 2, Peter Dobrin
wrote: "It was, along with a Symphony No. 1 that Wolfgang Sawallisch led at Tanglewood in 1999, one of the
greatest nights in recent years that this orchestra has had
with Brahms."[19] The lyricism, emotion, and refinement
that the Orchestra achieved with Muti gave great satisfaction to the admiring audience that filled Verizon Hall.
The possibility of Muti's future returns seems to have dis-
sipated any lingering resentment.

Soon after his reconquest of much of the Philadelphia
audience's and musicians' good will came the stunning
announcement of his resignation as the music director of
La Scala. Having received a vote of no confidence from
the La Scala musicians, who vowed to strike on the opening night of every production in the coming season, Muti
had no choice but to resign. He voiced his anger in his
public statement: "The hostility manifested in such a
coarse way by persons with whom I have worked for
almost 20 years makes it really impossible to carry on with
a relationship of collaboration, which ought to be based
on harmony and trust."[20]

After leaving his directorship of the Philadelphia Orchestra, Muti had chosen to give his greatest efforts to La Scala. Now there are years ahead for him to strengthen and expand his standing among the great conductors. Philadelphia audiences and musicians will take careful note of the accomplishments of his later years.

(previous) Wolfgang Sawallisch conducting. Reprinted by permission of
The Philadelphia Inquirer/John Costello

༄ Wolfgang Sawallisch ༄

Riccardo Muti's unexpected resignation left the Phil-adelphia Orchestra in the unusual position of scram-bling to find a music director in a relatively short period of time. Ormandy had been Stokowski's co-conductor for two years before his appointment as music director, and Muti was named permanent guest conductor some three years before his directorship. But now the Orchestra was faced with making a selection without day-to-day experi-ence with a conductor. A committee of 12 began its search in April 1990. Initially there were 230 candidates, who were subsequently narrowed down, first to 27 and then to 16. Five of these received six or more votes, including Wolfgang Sawallisch. From this group, a poll of musi-cians from the Orchestra chose Sawallisch. His guest appearances, with the warm relationship that he had forged with the Orchestra over the years, were to his advantage. At first the board remained somewhat hesi-tant. But because of the musicians' enthusiasm, they put out feelers to see what the music world thought of him. In addition, it was known that after Sawallisch's 1966 debut with the Orchestra, Ormandy had talked to him about becoming his successor and later had renewed the invitation. By that time, however, Sawallisch was the music director of the prestigious Bavarian State Opera in Munich, and he had declined.

Three members of the board flew to Munich to offer Sawallisch the position of music director. He told them that he and his wife had been thinking about something in the future with no administrative duties when his contract with the Bavarian Opera ended.[1] Nevertheless, he agreed to meet with them again. At this second meeting, in July 1990, 24 years after his first offer from Ormandy, he accepted the position of music director of the Philadelphia Orchestra.

Wolfgang Sawallisch was born on August 26, 1923, in Munich, Germany. He did not come from a family of musicians, but like all cultured Germans, his family loved music. Sawallisch writes in his autobiography[2] that his first musical memories are of his mother singing children's songs to him. On a visit to his paternal grandfather's home, he saw his first piano, and immediately he began to play the tunes that he had heard from his mother, to the point that his family had difficulty getting him away from the instrument. At his grandfather's urging, his parents bought him a piano, and he began private lessons at the age of five. At age 11 he heard his first opera, Humperdinck's *Hansel and Gretel*, in Munich's National Theater, and he was fascinated more by what the conductor was doing than by the action on stage. When he arrived home, he announced that although he would continue his piano lessons, what he really wanted to do was to conduct.

Around the age of 13 or 14, he saw Richard Strauss conduct a marvelous performance of Mozart's *Cosi Fan Tutte* in which the composer introduced certain themes from his own music that the audience immediately recognized as his little jokes. Sawallisch never met Strauss personally, but the memory of this performance always lasted.

Sawallisch attended the Wittelsbaucher High School of Music and, later, the Munich Conservatory, where he specialized in piano and composition under Wolfgang Ruoff and Hans Sachse. His studies were interrupted when he was drafted in 1942, at age 19, and stationed for six months of training in Augsburg. At one point he was temporarily released from army service and ordered to play on a radio station that was broadcasting classical music in an effort to bolster the public morale. After a month he returned to Augsburg to discover that his entire unit had been sent to Stalingrad. Not one man survived! In his autobiography Sawallisch expresses his gratitude to music for saving his life. Because of his musician's ears, he was sent to Italy, away from the front line, in order to handle Morse code as a radio operator. Eventually he was sent to the south of Italy, and there, in 1945, he was taken prisoner by the Americans and remained a POW for six months. When the war ended, he was free to return to Germany. He found his Munich in ruins. Fortunately the Munich Conservatory was able to function again, and he re-entered and completed his studies in 1946.

Sawallisch is one of the last conductors to follow in the German tradition of building his career slowly through a succession of opera houses and concert halls. In 1947 he became a répétiteur (accompanist, vocal coach, and chorus master) of the Augsburg Stadttheater, where he made his conducting debut and eventually became the principal conductor. In 1953, his last year there, he made a guest appearance with the Berlin Philharmonic, an orchestra with which he is still associated. At 30, he was the youngest conductor to lead this famed orchestra.

From 1953 to 1958, Sawallisch was the general music director of the Aachen Opera, once again, at 30, the youngest general music director in Germany. His direction of Wagnerian operas brought him an invitation to conduct at the Bayreuth Festival in 1957 in a new production of *Tristan und Isolde* (this time becoming the second-youngest person, after Richard Strauss, to conduct at Bayreuth). The opera was a huge success, followed by equal successes with *Lohengrin* (in 1958), with *Der Fliegende Holländer* (1959), and with *Tannhäuser* (1960). He became the music director of the Wiesbaden Opera (1958-60) and then music director of the Cologne Opera (1960-64). While in Cologne, he taught a course in conducting at the Cologne Academy of Music.

From 1961 until 1973, Sawallisch was the music director of the Hamburg Philharmonic Orchestra, and, at approximately the same time (1960-70), he held the same position with the Vienna Symphony Orchestra. With this latter orchestra he made his first appearance in the United States in 1964. In New York, before the U.S. tour began, the *New York Times* published an interview[3] in which Howard Klein described the 40-year-old German conductor in minute detail: his black hair and sharp widow's peak, his dark-rimmed glasses, small features, sturdy build – even the kind of suit and tie he was wearing. Sawallisch was in high spirits at the prospect of the orchestra's tour. He asked what encore might be appropriate for Bruckner's Symphony No. 3 and was surprised to learn that this European custom was not observed in the United States. During their five-week tour, which covered several American cities, Sawallisch impressed his audiences with his masterful performances of the German repertoire.

In 1966, as a direct result of the successful 1964 tour, he made his debut as guest conductor of the Philadelphia Orchestra in four concerts at the Academy of Music (March 3 to March 7) and, on March 8, in New York's Lincoln Center for the Performing Arts. His program consisted of Mozart's Symphony No. 38 in D Major, K 504 (*Prague*); Wolfgang Fortner's Symphony, 1947; and Schumann's Symphony No. 4 in D Minor, Op. 120. He has said that he was greatly affected by the famous "Philadelphia sound" and by the Orchestra's wonderful ability to play the music at the first reading. He returned as guest conductor in 1969 and throughout the 1980s.

From 1973 to 1980, Sawallisch was artistic director of the Orchestre de la Suisse Romande in Geneva. In 1971 he was appointed music director of the Bavarian State Opera in Munich, and he became its general manager in 1982. He led the world premiere of *Sim Tjong* by the Korean composer Isang Yun (1972), and in 1976 he conducted a new production of Wagner's *Ring Cycle* to celebrate the hundredth anniversary of its premiere. This was videotaped and later released in compact disc format.

Maestro Sawallisch regularly conducts the Vienna Symphony, the London Philharmonic, the Royal Concertgebouw Orchestra, the Orchestre National de France, and the NHK Orchestra in Tokyo. In addition, there are frequent guest appearances with the Berlin Philharmonic, the Vienna Philharmonic, the Israel Philharmonic, the Czech Philharmonic, and other major European orchestras. He conducts regularly at La Scala, Milan, and at the Vienna State Opera. Before his appointment as music director of the Philadelphia Orchestra, he had limited his guest conducting in the United States to San Francisco and Philadelphia.

In addition to his appearances at Bayreuth, he has conducted at festivals in Vienna, Salzburg, Edinburgh, Florence, Prague, Bregenz, Lucerne, and Montreux, and at the London Proms. Sawallisch is also a gifted pianist and performs frequently.

To date, he is the author of three books: *Stationen eines Dirigenten* ("Life Stages of a Conductor") published in Munich by Bruckmann in 1983; *Im Interesse de Deutlichkeit: Mein Leben mit der Musik* ("In the Interest of Clarity: My Life with Music"), published in Hamburg by Hoffmann und Campe in 1988; and *Kontrapunkt-Herausforderung Musik* ("Counterpoint – A Musical Challenge"), with the same publisher (1993).

The Philadelphia Orchestra was left without a music director for the 1992–93 season and became an orchestra of guest conductors and substitutes. To help alleviate this situation, Sawallisch, as music director–designate, flew to Philadelphia to be present for the opening night, and he returned for three weeks in February and March and for the last week of the subscription series. In total, he conducted eight subscription concerts, one concert in New York at Avery Fisher Hall, and the first of his "Come and Meet the Music" concerts, which he conducted and moderated. His comments during this event gave the audience a chance to savor his ironic Bavarian humor.

In May 1993, still as music director-designate, he led the Orchestra on their Asian tour. This first tour together started in Ichikawa (the first visit for the Orchestra), and continued to Sapporo, Tokyo, Mito, Beijing, Shanghai, and Hong Kong. In Tokyo the performance of Strauss became the first live recording by Sawallisch and the Philadelphia Orchestra. It was an auspicious beginning.

In the following September, at the official welcoming ceremony for Sawallisch and his wife, Mechthild, he said to the festive crowd, "We are Philadelphians." Obviously recalling President Kennedy's words in Berlin, he seemed, also, to be offering assurance that he would devote his primary efforts and attention to the Philadelphia Orchestra.

His opening week as the music director was a display of energy and stirring performances. The first concert was heavily weighted with American music: Aaron Copland's

Fanfare for the Common Man, followed by two works previously premiered by the Orchestra, Ned Rorem's *Eagles* and Samuel Barber's 1941 Violin Concerto No. 14, played by Itzhak Perlman. Brahms's Symphony No. 2 in D Major, Op. 73, which concluded the program, was a forceful rendition of one of Sawallisch's specialties. On Saturday morning he had his first Children's Concert, and that night he conducted Beethoven's Ninth Symphony to enthusiastic applause. On Sunday he joined the Philadelphia Orchestra Chamber Group for their opening concert in the Academy Ballroom.

In that first year (1993), he recorded Bruckner's Symphony No. 4 in E Flat (*Romantic*), and it is significant that in this early recording with the Orchestra, the reappearance of the "Philadelphia sound" was immediately hailed. This was a somewhat hasty appraisal, but in a short time critics and the public alike acknowledged the definite return of the lush string sound that had marked the Orchestra before Muti. In reality, this sound was not precisely as it had been, but heard after Muti's leaner sound, it seemed so with its fuller and richer quality. For Sawallisch the Orchestra played more robustly than under Muti, especially the strings, which regained their shimmering brilliance and glowing warmth. But Sawallisch kept the precision and balance that Muti had produced. Thus, the "Sawallisch sound" stands between the sound of the two former conductors and captures the distinctive qualities of both. It is a fascinating musical evolution.

It must have taken courage for a distinguished conductor of age 70, with a sterling reputation in Europe, to take on an American orchestra. Sawallisch, like many European conductors, was not familiar with what is expected of conductors in the United States – intimate and prodding press interviews, donor receptions, autograph signing, involvement with women's auxiliaries, publicity stunts, and so on. He really knew very little about life in the United States, and Americans must have seemed brash to this reserved and courtly gentleman who possessed such personal dignity. He was undaunted, however, by American customs and expectations. He obviously found his new environment invigorating, and he entered into his many duties with zeal. He gave his first and complete loyalty to the Philadelphia Orchestra and arranged his active international career around this commitment.

Sawallisch's conducting technique is reserved and courtly, like his personality. There are no affectations, no posturing. Upon entering the stage, he gives the impression that he is scarcely aware of the audience; the important thing is to get to his Orchestra and begin the music. With a clean baton technique, he uses a minimum of conducting gestures, but every gesture is meaningful. He is the opposite of a Bernstein or a Stokowski, because he

Wolfgang Sawallisch at a Verizon Hall rehearsal. Reprinted by permission of
The Philadelphia Inquirer/Gerald S. Williams

believes – and acts upon this belief – that the music is what is important and that the conductor is not there to entertain. He has no desire to be a celebrity conductor, and his calm exterior is sometimes misread by the audience, which has criticized the supposed lack of drama. Now that it is possible in Verizon Hall to face the conductor from the conductor's circle, his subtle signals to the Orchestra can be observed: his sensitive facial expressions, the raising of an eyebrow, his eye contact with the players, a small smile of encouragement or approval, the quick look of displeasure, plus the constant use of intricate left-hand cues. There is such rapport between conductor and musicians that these subtleties are immediately understood and result in complete ensemble unity. (Maestro Sawallisch has acknowledged that he is not a particular fan of the seats behind the stage because, he says, there are moments when he would prefer not to have any intrusion between the Orchestra and himself. The players say that he has toned down some of his most expressive facial expressions as a result of the new seating arrangement.) Audiences in the theater seats can see many of the graceful left-hand indications, especially to the violins, and hear the occasional stomp of his feet to jump-start the Orchestra. At the end of any piece, Sawallisch almost seems to bow to his Orchestra before he turns to the audience. And the applause is always shared with his "colleagues."

His preparation for every performance is faultless, as is his knowledge of every score that he conducts. In his closed rehearsals, he shapes the music carefully, but he does not tear it all apart, nor does he rehash something with which the players are completely familiar. He trusts his musicians. Because of his confidence in the music, in the players, and even in the sophistication of the audience, he can produce introspection and depth where another interpretation might be more flashy. He has the ability to inspire the musicians to play their best. He is able to evoke great emotion from the Orchestra, or communicate the wit and humor in a Haydn or a Mendelssohn. The interpretation is always his, but he also allows the players a certain freedom of expression that results in spontaneity and freshness.

In rehearsals open to the public, Sawallisch follows the European custom of considering them as final run-throughs with few, if any, interruptions. He had already shaped the music in the closed rehearsals. In the Academy the audience could sit in the front rows, and a very rare comment might be overheard. In Verizon Hall, the first 12 rows are cordoned off, but occasionally Sawallisch's very pleasant voice can be heard singing to illustrate the effect he wants.

In these public rehearsals, the maestro enters the stage like one of the players. Next to the podium there is always a wooden valet. He takes off his suit coat, hangs it up carefully, and in shirt, tie, and sweater-vest proceeds to sit down and conduct. At the intermission, he puts on the suit coat and walks off stage. The exact procedure is repeated at the beginning and end of the second part of the rehearsal. It has the quality of an Old World ritual, and it became endearing to the audience because it was so natural to him.

Sawallisch was a vigorous 70 when he began his leadership of the Orchestra. Even so, the management felt somewhat wary about presenting this stalwart German septuagenarian to the public after the dashing Italian. His acceptance by the players was immediate – and grew enormously – but complete acceptance by the audiences came slowly. In addition to the public's normal wait-and-see attitude, he met some opposition in segments of the Jewish community who questioned his activity in the German army. Sawallisch was aware of this animosity, which greatly distressed him, and to clear up the unfounded suspicions and rumors about his war record, he consented to an interview on the topic with the *Jewish Exponent*.[4] He spoke quite freely about his army service, and he stressed the fact that he was never a member of the Nazi party (which the U.S. State Department has confirmed). He said that as he was in the infantry, he had no idea of the actions of the Nazis, nor any concept of the existence of concentration camps. Only after the war had ended did he and his family discover the horror and the suffering unleashed by Hitler on the Jewish people. "I regret what happened between the Germans and the Jewish people during those awful times. . . . maybe music can help both Germans and Jews to overcome the terrible past."

Some Jews thought that his statement calling it "stupid for Germany, a small country, to do battle with such a major power as Russia" showed that he was oblivious to the greater horror of the war. On the other hand, some supporters of Sawallisch felt that requiring him to endure questions about his wartime past was a form of discrimination. Sawallisch himself pointed out that there were many Jews in the Orchestra, and everyone knew that he was German. Yet "they asked me to be their Music Director." Most Jews eventually came to accept the fact that, like young men everywhere, he was drafted without subscribing to the politics or ideology of the war. Throughout his years in Philadelphia, Sawallisch made sensitive efforts to quell doubts about his sincerity and about his hatred of war.

Sawallisch is one of the greatest living representatives of the German-Austrian and Central European repertoires. Nevertheless, with the Philadelphia Orchestra he expanded his repertoire considerably. His world premieres championed contemporary music. He added American composers and took this music on tour. He also brought more sacred music into the concert hall: for example Schubert's Sixth Mass, Verdi's *Requiem*, Mendelssohn's *Elijah*, and Beethoven's *Missa Solemnis*[5] (last performed by Ormandy in 1967).

Above all, he offered Richard Strauss throughout his programming. He staged a concert version of Strauss's opera *Ariadne auf Naxos*,[6] which had particular success in Carnegie Hall (1995). His performance of Strauss's *Metamorphosen*, which suggested the chaos of postwar Germany, and the poignant *Death and Transfiguration*, which brought tears to many in the audience, illuminated the beauty and depth of Strauss's music. The maestro's unusual statement early in his tenure that Strauss was "the most significant musical figure of the 20th century"[7] piqued the interest of many scholars, some of whom came to hold this view after hearing Sawallisch's interpretations of Strauss's music in performances and recordings.

Maestro Sawallisch often programmed a season with emphasis on a particular composer. The 1994–95 season featured Haydn. There was a Beethoven festival in 1995–96, a season-long celebration of Brahms in 1996–97, and a three-week "Orchestra Virtuosi Festival" in 1997–98. The anniversary season, 2000–2001, featured music written during the Orchestra's lifetime, in particular by composers closely associated with the

Orchestra. At first, misunderstanding what would be included in this twentieth-century music, the public balked at the idea of expected dissonance and atonal offerings. But when the actual programs were announced, there was a reversal of opinion, and the season proved to be very successful.

In 2002–3, his last season as music director, Sawallisch featured the music of Robert Schumann: 14 subscription concerts, four concerts at Carnegie Hall, two chamber music concerts. Robert and Clara Schumann's lieder occupied one half of a special concert performed by Thomas Hampson, baritone, and Wolfgang Sawallisch, pianist. Live performances of Schumann's music became the first CDs to be recorded in the Kimmel Center.

Sawallisch has put his indelible stamp on the Orchestra for many years to come through the 40 players whom he engaged (plus one conductor-in-residence and two assistant conductors) – approximately one-third of the Orchestra. His appointments have added superb musicians, and the impact is particularly felt because so many are principal players, including trumpet, viola, harp, trombone, bassoon, double bass, clarinet, and concertmaster. Four associate principals and two assistant principals are part of this group. The maestro's last appointment – principal clarinetist – came to the Orchestra from the same position in the Metropolitan Opera Orchestra.

Finding a suitable concertmaster caused difficulties for Sawallisch. The very fine violinist Norman Carol, who had been the concertmaster since the Ormandy regime, developed a severe nerve problem in his neck, which affected his playing so that he could not continue. Erez Ofer was engaged. Everyone agreed that he was a splendid violinist, but, unfortunately, unconcerned with the duties of concertmaster. He was never given tenure, and Sawallisch had to let him go. The most recent concertmaster, David Kim, is both an excellent violinist and a committed concertmaster.

Typical of his spirit of collegiality, Sawallisch never seeks the limelight. With the many soloists that he brought to the stage, he always stepped back after their performances in order to direct the applause to them rather than to himself. Well-known singers and instrumentalists who have performed with Sawallisch and the Philadelphia Orchestra include André Watts, Sarah Chang, Thomas Hampson, Lang Lang, Hillary Hahn, Murray Perahia, Midori, András Schiff, Gil Shaham, Dawn Upshaw, Maurizio Pollini, Christoph Eschenbach, Barbara Hendricks, Radu Lupu, Garrick Ohlsson, Rudolf Buchbinder, Leónidas Kavakos, Yefin Bronfman, Emanuel Ax, Itzhak Perlman, Yo-Yo Ma, and many others.

The maestro's frequent appearances as pianist added another facet to the Sawallisch era. Whether he served as pianist-conductor, accompanist of soloists, or chamber musician, his performances formed a tangible link with the Orchestra members. A sensitive, beautiful pianist, he understood what it meant to be a performer. Ormandy, a good violinist, gave up performing and dedicated himself entirely to conducting. Muti often rehearsed at the piano with singers, but appeared only once as pianist with the Orchestra chamber musicians. Sawallisch, on the other hand, was a well-known chamber musician and accompanist in Europe who performed and recorded with leading instrumentalists and singers, and he continued these activities in Philadelphia. He was generous with his performances outside the Orchestra, for example: in annual performances with the Wistar Quartet at the German Society;[8] with the Pasquale String Quartet; in concert at Temple University's Rock Hall with violinist William de Pasquale; in concert with the Russian baritone Dmitri Hvorostovsky in the Academy Ballroom; in a program of lieder with Thomas Hampson. And for eight years he appeared with the Philadelphia Orchestra Chamber Music series. He said it was wonderful to be involved in performing, and it was obvious that he loved his role as pianist.

The most impressive of his pianistic feats came in what is now known as "the legendary winter concert of 1994." To launch his opera offerings, he had scheduled four

Wolfgang Sawallisch at the piano. Courtesy of Joanna Lightner

concerts of excerpts from Wagner's *Tannhäuser* and *Die Walküre*. The first three concerts were great successes, but on Friday, February 11, the night of the fourth concert, Philadelphia was snowbound. It became obvious that many musicians who lived outside the city would not be able to travel in to the Academy, and everyone expected an announcement that the concert would be canceled. Sawallisch had other plans. The three soloists – soprano Deborah Voigt, tenor Heikki Siukola, and bass René Papa – were staying in Center City hotels. The chorus, the Philadelphia Singers Chorale, was also available nearby. So he himself would play the Orchestra's part! Word spread through the city, and by 8:00 P.M. there was a crowd of around six hundred. "You are witnessing a very unusual event," Sawallisch told the audience, which had moved closer to the stage. "This is my world premiere opera in-concert version on piano. Let's see what happens."[9] Conducting from the piano, and inserting words of explanation here and there, he captivated his audience. It established Sawallisch as a virtuosic pianist, a master of ingenuity, and an all-around good sport. And it deeply endeared him to the Philadelphia community.

The maestro conducted 47 Philadelphia Orchestra "firsts." To express his own horror of war, he chose for the first of these performances (October 1993) Benjamin Britten's powerful *War Requiem*. (On stage after the October 14 performance, Sawallisch and others held a brief discussion of the work.) Also heard for the first time in Philadelphia were several compositions by Strauss, Schubert, Bach, Haydn, Mozart, Hindemith, Kurt Weill, Carl Maria von Weber, and Henryk Górecki.

Sawallisch programmed 34 world and U.S. premieres, of which he himself conducted 13 world and two U.S. premieres. The world premieres were:

Jacob Druckman, *Counterpoise*, 1993–94
Bernard Rands, *Canzoni per Orchestra*, 1994–95
Viktor Ullmann, Symphony No. 1, 1994–95
(Written at the Theresienstadt concentration camp by the Jewish composer Viktor Ullmann, who died at Auschwitz, this work was performed on the anniversary of the date on which the Allied soldiers entered Auschwitz.)
George Rochberg, Clarinet Concerto, 1995–96
Wolfgang Rihm, *Ernster Gesang*, 1996–97
Roland Pöntinen, *Blue Winter* (trombone and string orchestra), 1997–98
Daniel Dorff, *Three Fun Fables*, 1999–2000
Einojuhani Rautavaara, Symphony No. 8 (*The Journey*), 1999–2000
Huang Ruo, *Three Pieces for Orchestra* (third movement), 2000–2001

Roberto Sierra, *Concierto para orquesta*, 2001–2 (This was composed in conjunction with a residency at the Potter Thomas Elementary School in North Philadelphia, part of an effort by the Orchestra to interest Puerto Rican and other Hispanic children in classical music.)

Aaron Jay Kernis, *Color Wheel*, 2001–2

Jennifer Higdon, Concerto for Orchestra, 2001–2

Krzysztof Penderecki, Piano Concerto *(Resurrection)*, 2001–2[10]

The Orchestra's U.S. premiers were:

Wagner, Symphony in E Major, 1994–95

William Mathias, *Helios*, 1995–96

The year 2000 was the Orchestra's one hundredth anniversary, which was celebrated throughout the year in a series of performances, tours, publications, broadcasts, a competition, and eight commissioned works.

On October 5, having reviewed 330 entries in the composition competition, Sawallisch and the Orchestra performed the works of the three finalists: Kevin Beavers, Keith Fitch, and Huang Ruo. The audience and Orchestra members voted for the winner, Mr. Beavers, whose composition was played for the remainder of the weekend and in Carnegie Hall.

On October 11, 2000, honoring both its one hundredth space shuttle launch and the Orchestra's one hundredth anniversary, NASA presented a videotape of the Orchestra performing Richard Strauss's *Also Sprach Zarathustra*. The shuttle *Discovery* carried the baton that Wolfgang Sawallisch had used during the taping earlier in September. (Thus the Orchestra can boast among its "firsts" that it was the first symphony orchestra officially represented in space.)

The Orchestra Birthday Gala, a glittering evening of celebration of the Orchestra's 100 years, was held in the Academy of Music, its original home, on November 16, 2000. Seen on international television, the program included Toccata and Fugue in D Minor, by Johann Sebastian Bach, orchestrated by Leopold Stokowski; *The Sorcerer's Apprentice*, by Paul Dukas; Piano Concerto No. 2 in C Minor, Op. 18, by Sergei Rachmaninoff (André Watts, soloist); Fantasy on Bizet's *Carmen* (for violin and orchestra), Op. 25, by Pablo Sarasate (Sarah Chang, soloist); *Old American Songs* by Aaron Copland (Thomas Hampson, baritone); and Suite from *Firebird* (1919 version) by Igor Stravinsky.

Later in the season, the Orchestra offered a free concert in Rittenhouse Square as a "Centennial Gift to the City."

The eight commissioned works were performed over three seasons. Among these were Roberto Sierra's

Concierto para orquesta, heard in February 2001; Aaron Jay Kernis's *Color Wheel,* chosen by Sawallisch for the formal opening of the Kimmel Center, December 15, 2001; and Jennifer Higdon's Concerto for Orchestra, peculiarly suited to the acoustics of Verizon Hall and performed for the last concert in honor of the centennial, June 2002.

There were other highlights in Sawallisch's years as music director. One of the most unforgettable was the concert at the Mann Center after the disaster of September 11. Sawallisch was in Europe, but in order to be with the American city and the Orchestra that he loved, he drove to Munich in the pre-dawn hours and boarded the first plane out of Germany. He arrived in time for one rehearsal before the free concert on September 16, a concert of consolation and hope, which was multicast to more than twenty U.S. cities on WHYY-TV and FM. It was a deeply moving tribute for which everyone concerned had donated his or her efforts.

Variegated activities crowded Sawallisch's days. There were town meetings; a WFLN 1993 radiothon; a 1997 live cybercast of a concert on the internet (the first by a major orchestra); a 1997 concert in front of Independence Hall during the President's Summit for America's Future; a joint concert with the Israel Philharmonic in 1998; a concert by the Curtis Student Symphony Orchestra,

Sawallisch conducting. Reprinted by permission of The Philadelphia Inquirer/
Akira Suwa

which he conducted in the Academy of Music; the inauguration of free neighborhood concerts in 2000; auditions, preconcert discussions, performance commentaries, and constant interviews.

His annual Saturday morning Family Concert (formerly known as the Children's Concert) was surprisingly successful, particularly his first one, in 1993, where he discussed Strauss's *Till Eulenspiegel* with the children and then performed it with the Orchestra. The children were always fascinated by this engaging grandfatherly figure who spoke to them so enthusiastically. (The clown who addressed the children in the 2002 concert, with a wordless Sawallisch conducting the Orchestra, was a great disappointment.)

Mr. Sawallisch is the recipient of many honors. He is an honorary member and honorary conductor of the Vienna Symphony Orchestra and of the Hamburg Philharmonic; the only honorary conductor laureate of the NHK Symphony Orchestra in Tokyo (where he has appeared as guest conductor every year since 1964); and honorary member of the Accademia di Santa Cecilia (Rome). Sawallisch was the first non-Italian conductor to be awarded the coveted Toscanini Gold Baton in recognition of his 35-year association with La Scala (November 1993). He received the Austrian Prize for Art and Knowledge in 1997.

In 1993 *Musical America* named him "Conductor of the Year." He received the Union League tribute in 1994 and the Penn Club tribute in 1997 (both Philadelphia awards). In 2000 he received the Pennsylvania Governor's Distinguished Arts Award.[11] He is the recipient of the Avatar Award for Artistic Excellence from the Arts and Business Council of Philadelphia. He has honorary doctorates from the Curtis Institute of Music, the Westminster Choir College of Rider University, and Villanova University.

Maestro Sawallisch's discography is notable.[12] One of his releases is Strauss's *Die Frau Ohne Schatten*, the first uncut version of the opera, which won several international awards, including the Grand Prix de l'Académie Charles Cros and the Prix Cecilia. In 1990 his video release of Wagner's complete *Der Ring des Nibelungen* received the German Video Winner Special Prize, and in 1993 he was the recipient of *Gramophone*'s "Concerto of the Year" Award for Brahms's Piano Concerto No. 2 in B Flat Major, Op. 83, with the London Philharmonic and soloist Stephen Kovacevich. In 1995 his EMI Hindemith CD, recorded with the Philadelphia Orchestra, won the Cannes Classical Award for "Best Orchestral Recording of 19th and 20th Century Music." It also won a Grammy nomination for the "Best Orchestra Performance." The Schumann CD with the Philadelphia Orchestra (the first recording in Verizon Hall) was nominated for two

Grammy awards and received the *New York Times* "Best of 2003 Award."

With the Philadelphia Orchestra, he has 70 recordings. The Bruckner Symphony No. 4 in E Flat (*Romantic*), which he recorded with the Orchestra in his first year (1993), is considered one of the finest recordings of this work. Sawallisch is the pianist-conductor of Beethoven's *Choral Fantasy*, and there are five more recordings made in Philadelphia in which Sawallisch is the pianist:

Robert Schumann, Piano Quintet in E flat Major, Op. 44 (fourth movement), 1993

Wagner, *Tannhäuser*, Act 2, excerpts, with soloists and chorus, 1994

Wagner, *Die Walküre*, Act 2, with soloists, 1994

Robert Schumann, *Andante and Variations*, with Buchbinder and chamber group, 2003

Clara Schumann, *Five Songs*, with Thomas Hampson, 2003

In spite of his extensive discography, Sawallisch is not a big enthusiast for studio recording. He speaks of the "beautiful task" of focusing on the actual moment of interpretation with complete concentration on the music and without the possibility of later corrections.

Even so, Sawallisch is pragmatic enough to understand the benefit to the Orchestra of recordings. The

Philadelphia Orchestra had once been a major recording orchestra, and the cancellation of the EMI contract in 1996, after an association of almost 80 years, was a severe blow. Because of the lower costs of recording in Europe, fewer and fewer companies will record in the United States. The Orchestra has responded by using smaller and less well known companies – for example, Water-Lily Acoustics (for the CD *Nature's Realm*) – and by recording under their own auspices (The Philadelphia Orchestra Association: POA).

In addition to the cancellation of the EMI contract, there was the distressingly long nine-week strike that began on September 16, 1996. The management, facing a three-year deficit, wanted to reduce the musicians' benefits. The musicians wanted an increase in both pay and health benefits. Already upset about the EMI cancellation and the suspension of radio and television broadcasts,[13] they were also angry about the delay in building a new concert hall. Sawallisch was devastated by the bitterness of this conflict. He kept silent as he had promised, although this was very difficult for him, and he endured the slings of critics just as Ormandy had when he did not take sides. While Sawallisch certainly understood the issues that the musicians faced, there were intimations that he had difficulty reconciling his commitment to music with the idea of striking. Putting the music in second place would have gone against his work ethic. Fortunately, when the strike was over and Sawallisch returned to his podium, the mutual respect and devotion between conductor and musicians was quickly restored.

After the initial 1993 tour to Asia, Sawallisch conducted at least one tour every season. He took great pride in showing off the Orchestra. On these trips he was indefatigable, still cheerful and energetic when others were showing fatigue. Once asked about the effects of jet lag, he replied, "I do not have jet lag." The 1994 tour began in Chicago and went on to Mexico, Brazil, Argentina, and Chile. The performance in Aguascalientes in Mexico marked the Orchestra's first visit there. Another tour in 1994 concentrated on five American cities. In 1995 the Orchestra visited Europe: London, Frankfurt, Lucerne, Salzburg, Berlin, and, for the first time, Montreaux. The next year (1996) saw the Orchestra in five cities in Asia. The two-week tour of 10 European cities in 1997 included Venice for the first time. The extensive tour of 1998 began in California and reached Mexico, Brazil, Argentina, and Chile. In Mexico City they had to project the concert on screens outside the Palacio de Bellas Artes in order to accommodate the overflow audience.

It was Asia again in 1999, a tour to seven cities, among these four that were new for the Orchestra: Hanoi, Ho Chi Minh City, Taipei, and Kuala Lumpur (with the first internet chat). Governor Tom Ridge accompanied them on this first visit of an American symphony orchestra to Vietnam. (Joining in the festive mood before the trip, Ridge played the bass drum in the rehearsal where the press was present.) Many Orchestra players remember vividly the outreach to the children of Hanoi and the emotions felt when they played the American national anthem.

In 2000 the Orchestra traveled to Europe and played in 12 cities. It was the first visit to Leipzig and Bergamo. The Orchestra's concert in Cologne, recorded live for a DVD,[14] was transmitted to huge television screens mounted outside the famous cathedral. The program consisted of Rautavaara's Symphony No. 8 (*The Journey*) and Strauss's Symphonia Domestica, Op. 53. The first received polite applause, but for Strauss (and Sawallisch) there was an ovation.

The year 2000 also saw a five-city tour of the U.S. South, with West Palm Beach receiving its first visit. In 2001 there was an Asian tour of eight cities (Toyama was new for the Orchestra). An additional 2001 tour of 12 U.S. cities (Iowa City was new) turned out to be Sawallisch's last with the Orchestra. No tour had been scheduled for 2002, and in 2003 his illness prevented him from making the final tour of his 10-year term.

Sawallisch said on more than one occasion that there was no more satisfying experience than reading a score. The sound, the rhythm, the balance are all perfect in the imagination. While it is usually impossible to translate all this into reality, he has stated, with obvious admiration, that an orchestra of the quality of the Philadelphia Orchestra allows you to produce what you imagine.[15]

Although idealistic in every sense, Sawallisch can also be down to earth. In a listing of the personal "interests" of the Orchestra members (in a publication in honor of the Orchestra's one hundredth anniversary), Sawallisch gave his "interests" as "piano, studying music scores, gardening."[16] But the players knew that his additional "interest" was gadgetry and that his favorite place in the Philadelphia area was the Home Depot. In his home in Germany he has a workshop, where he likes to fix clocks, radios, and electrical appliances. One musician said that if he should ever come to your home, he would probably tinker with the light switches.

Such human elements complement the portrait of a methodical, disciplined conductor who, since 1945, has kept a notebook with details of every rehearsal and concert that he conducts, together with his analysis of each one.

It is known that the maestro works hard on his English, and few would ever correct him. On the other hand, if someone tries to speak German to him, his or her mistakes will be corrected immediately.

During the last program at the Academy, Sawallisch's baton somehow broke in two, with one part flying into the

Orchestra. With his customary calmness, he put the remaining part into his pocket and continued conducting with his hands.

Sawallisch and his wife made their home in Grassau, Germany, and lived in an apartment at the Rittenhouse during the months when they were in Philadelphia. They became good Philadelphians, just as the maestro had promised at the outset of his tenure.

When Sawallisch was guest-conducting the Israel Philharmonic in 1997, he and his wife visited the Chaim Sheba Medical Center in Tel Hashomer. Upon their return to Philadelphia, Mrs. Sawallisch initiated a support group, Friends of Sheba. After her death, Sawallisch continued her efforts by organizing concerts in Philadelphia and New York to benefit the Medical Center. Outstanding artists such as Gil Shaham, Emanuel Ax, Yefim Bronfman, and Sarah Chang donated their talents.

Mechthild Sawallisch always accompanied her husband. She was with him on all the tours, and she could be seen in the audience of the Academy whenever he conducted. In an article in the *Philadelphia Inquirer*, Sawallisch said that he fell in love with her when he was 16 and she 18, when he was her accompanist and she was singing on the radio.[17] In his autobiography he writes tenderly of her beautiful soprano voice and of her accomplishments as a musician: "She sacrificed her career for our love."[18] They were married after the war, and they have one son, Georg.

In August 1998, to celebrate her husband's seventy-fifth birthday, Mrs. Sawallisch planned a surprise dinner and concert that included several guests from abroad. Unexpectedly, Sawallisch had to host his own birthday fete because his wife was in the hospital. Although he knew that she had been diagnosed with cancer, he nevertheless returned to Philadelphia to fulfill his fall commitments to the Orchestra. When her condition worsened, he canceled his performances for the last two weeks in October and went back to Germany to be at her side. Mechthild Sawallisch died during Christmas week, 1998.[19] After 46 years of an extremely close marriage, Sawallisch returned alone to Philadelphia for his scheduled concerts beginning in January 1999. Nothing was canceled, not one rehearsal, not one concert. Reports say that he became even closer to his Orchestra. In turn, they watched him grapple stoically with his sorrow and loneliness. Only once, in his first week back, during a rehearsal of the funereal Adagio of Bruckner's Sixth Symphony, did his emotions break through.

Music was Sawallisch's solace. He can become passionate in speaking of music as an expression of the human desire for harmony and beauty. In an interview on German television, he said: "I am still convinced that music, more than any other art, brings together people of all continents, all races, and all groups of society. I cannot imagine a life without it."[20]

As part of his civic leadership, Sawallisch became a crucial advocate for a new hall for the Orchestra, and his strong approval helped make a convincing case for building the Kimmel Center for the Performing Arts. He may have been a representative of Old World gentility, but he was very modern in his understanding of contemporary public relations. He accepted the necessity of a structure that would serve for different kinds of performances and not exclusively for the symphony. Sharing his vast experience of concert halls, he spent many hours with the architect and the acousticians.

Sawallisch must have been uncomfortable with the hijinks of the televised preview concert that introduced the Kimmel Center to the public on December 14, 2001. Nevertheless, he consented to conduct the brass section of the Orchestra in Copland's *Fanfare for the Common Man*. In discussing the propriety of the rest of the opening night, which included dubious duets by Sidney Kimmel and Paul Anka, plus two hours of Elton John, some Orchestra members are still outspoken in their disapproval, and one or two believe that Muti would never have had anything to do with such tastelessness. On the next night, Saturday, December 15, was the formal Gala

Inaugural Concert, broadcast nationally on WHYY, TV12 and FM. The varied program consisted of Kernis's *Color Wheel*, Ravel's *Daphnis et Chloé*, and the highlight of the evening, Beethoven's Triple Concerto in C Major, Op. 56, with Emanuel Ax, Itzhak Perlman, and Yo-Yo Ma together with the Orchestra. (When Yo-Yo Ma kept right on playing his cello as his chair fell backward off his platform and into the violin section, the television cameras caught Sawallisch's expression of inner mirth.)

Playing in Verizon Hall, the Orchestra's new home within the Kimmel Center, proved to be very different from playing in the Academy. The acoustics of the open-spaced new hall allow a more brilliant sound and expose every note, as opposed to the closed-in space of the Academy, with its more forgiving acoustics. At first it was disconcerting for the players to be able to hear each orchestra section so clearly, and they have had to learn to play and blend in a different way. There is still a lingering difference of opinion among the musicians about the relative merits of the two halls. A few say that in Verizon Hall the sound is generic, making the Philadelphia Orchestra seem like every other orchestra. In achieving more clarity, they feel that the quality of the sound is more like that which is heard through up-to-date speakers. Other musicians rejoice precisely in the clarity of tone in Verizon Hall. Acousticians maintain a continuous debate about perfecting the acoustics. Maestro Sawallisch has called it a dangerous hall, but he has said that he is pleased with the outcome, and it is evident that he enjoys performing there. A review in the *Philadelphia Inquirer* during Sawallisch's second season as conductor laureate stated: "Funny, Verizon Hall's acoustical troubles seem to go away when Sawallisch is here . . . even the hall falls into line."[21]

In the late 1990s, Maestro Sawallisch indicated his desire to retire as music director whenever his successor could be selected. He said that he wanted to stay until the completion of the Kimmel Center, and he added that he hoped always to be associated in some way with "his beloved Orchestra." Simon Rattle was everyone's first choice for the new music director, but it was not possible to lure him to the position. In January 2001, Christoph Eschenbach was named music director–designate, to begin in the 2003–4 season. In interviews in Europe Eschenbach seemed to suggest that he would change the famous "Philadelphia sound," but later he stated that this was a misunderstanding, that he meant he did not want this sound for every composer. Always gracious, Sawallisch has said that Eschenbach is right for the Orchestra in the twenty-first century. He added that new attempts to bring classical music closer to the public and reach out to different audiences must take the present into account.

The last weeks of the 2003 season were plagued with health problems for Sawallisch. Instead of the usual sturdy and reliable presence, there were last-minute cancellations and substitute conductors. Suffering from orthostatic hypotension, extreme fluctuation of blood pressure, and resultant overwhelming fatigue and dizziness, he needed to be seated while conducting – if he was able to appear on stage at all. Because he was known for his limitless energy and stamina, this change was deeply disappointing and sad for Sawallisch, for his Orchestra, and for the audience. The final concerts on Wednesday, Friday, and Saturday were to have been gala events to celebrate a splendid decade. Instead, there was an anxious tension. On Wednesday night the television screens on either side of the stage lit up with a film tribute to Wolfgang Sawallisch. To begin the program, David Hayes, music director of the Philadelphia Singers Chorale, conducted Brahms's *Song of Destiny*.

Did that mean that Sawallisch could not conduct the Beethoven? A long pause brought the hall to complete silence. When Sawallisch did appear, the audience greeted him in a standing ovation. Beethoven's Symphony No. 9 burst forth with all its majesty. It was a repetition of the program that Sawallisch had offered 10 years before during his first week as music director. Even the chorus and chorus master were the same. Sawallisch leaned against a stool as he conducted, but he was in complete control of the music. At the end, the audience saluted him with shouts of "Bravo," four curtain calls, and another standing ovation. The gala dinner in his honor followed the concert on Wednesday. Sawallisch needed to rest for an hour before he could join the festivities, but he was able to do so and to give a short, moving speech that ended: "I've had the great experience to make music with the best musicians in the world. I speak to you [the musicians present] and you understand me. I love you." Sadly, he was unable to make his last tour with the Orchestra. Instead, he left immediately for Germany and further medical treatment.

Sawallisch was named conductor laureate, and if his health permits, he will conduct several concerts in Philadelphia each year. He is also scheduled for many guest-conducting appearances around the world.

In his new role of conductor laureate, he has returned to Philadelphia in January 2004 and in February 2005. He is still battling physical weakness and he must sit to conduct, but his commanding presence on the podium remains the same. His initial program in 2004 consisted of Bruckner's Symphony No. 5 in B Flat Major, which was also performed in Carnegie Hall. A review in the *New York Times* praised Sawallisch's "calmly authoritative and altogether mesmerizing performance of Bruckner's daunting

Fifth Symphony. It was clear from this performance that the devoted players are eager to have Mr. Sawallisch return as long and as often as he can."[22] His performances in 2005 brought the highest accolades from his musicians, audiences, and critics.

There is general agreement that Sawallisch has been the conductor most beloved by the members of the Orchestra. Their affection begins with Sawallisch's respect and admiration for them. Although he is the authority figure, there has always been a great sense of partnership. To him the players are his peers, his colleagues. "*We* are the Philadelphia Orchestra," he often commented. The musicians admire his artistic integrity, the depth of his musicianship, his great culture, and the inspiration of his selfless commitment to the Orchestra. Early on they had discovered the warmth, charm, and wry wit beneath his inherent dignity and decorum. The musicians were doubly touched that such a private, formal person was so openly expressive of his affection for them, and they knew that it was genuine. The majority of tributes in his gala book are an outpouring of affection and appreciation from the members of the Orchestra to a musicians' musician.

At the end of Sawallisch's tenure as music director of the Philadelphia Orchestra, a blending of the Old World and the New, of German and American, had come about.

Both Sawallisch and the Orchestra benefited from this fusion. When Sawallisch became the music director, he was an established, greatly respected musician, esteemed throughout Europe. His decade with the Orchestra added a glorious chapter to his career and to the history of the Philadelphia Orchestra.

༼ᗉ Voices from the Music World ᗉ༽

Gary Graffman, Lang Lang, Sarah Chang

The interaction of soloists and conductors is always fascinating. Among the numerous soloists who have performed with the Philadelphia Orchestra, Gary Graffman, Lang Lang, and Sarah Chang have especially strong ties to the Philadelphia scene, and therefore a special relationship with the Orchestra and its music directors. Taken together, these artists span the eras of Maestros Ormandy, Muti, and Sawallisch.

Gary Graffman, pianist, was a frequent soloist with Eugene Ormandy and performed once with Riccardo Muti. Since 1986 he has been the president/director of the Curtis Institute of Music, where his contact with the conductors takes a different form. He will retire from Curtis in 2006. Lang Lang, also a pianist, came to Philadelphia from China at age 14 to study at Curtis. He made his Philadelphia debut with Wolfgang Sawallisch and the Orchestra in the Academy of Music and then performed with them during their 2001 tour of Asia. Violinist Sarah

Chang, born in Philadelphia, made her Philadelphia debut at age 10 with Riccardo Muti and has played many times with Maestro Sawallisch.

These musicians graciously consented to be interviewed about their experiences with the music directors. Their concepts and thoughts shed light on the relationship between conductor and soloist and add a further dimension to the portraits of the "Philadelphia Maestros."

Interview with G A R Y   G R A F F M A N

Pianist and President/
Director of the Curtis Institute of Music

Q. You have been the soloist many times with Eugene Ormandy and the Philadelphia Orchestra.[1] How would you describe the relationship between Ormandy, the conductor, and the soloist?

A. Ormandy was known by everyone as the best accompanist among the great conductors. I would say there were no exceptions. If someone asked you who do you think is the best accompanist, Ormandy's name would come up immediately. He was amazing, as if he anticipated what you were going to do, even if in a performance you played something slightly differently. A great chamber musician would have this ability as well. Ormandy's ability came from something in his brain. It was simply amazing. There was never a problem or a question when you were the soloist.

Q. In 1988 you performed with Riccardo Muti in the Academy of Music, playing Ravel's Piano Concerto for the Left Hand. How would you describe the manner in which Muti collaborated with soloists?

A. Although I got to know Muti personally, that was the only time I performed with him. Before the first rehearsal you got together to determine any place in the music where there might be a sudden change in tempo. He would want to know how the soloist does the *ritardando* and *accelerando*, and anything that the soloist has had experience in. This was really a normal piano rehearsal.

And then, because of union regulations, you are limited in how much rehearsal time you have. The usual standard is a maximum of two rehearsals, and the second is really a play-through. If the conductor likes the soloist – and if not, he wouldn't have engaged him, or at least won't engage him again – he goes over the piece, stops when necessary, and goes over that part. Both Muti and Sawallisch were excellent collaborators. After all, both have done so much opera. We are talking of the highest at the highest levels.

Q. In case the conductor and soloist disagree, who has the final word?

A. It often depends on age. This sounds as if I am joking, but it does depend on who is older. If a mature conductor engages a young, talented 18-year-old soloist, probably the conductor will prevail. If it's a young conductor, and he has engaged a middle-aged or older soloist, it is the opposite. For example, I started to play with orchestras when I was very young, 17; and for Szell and Ormandy, I was "little Gary." The first time I played with a younger conductor — by my standards today, I was quite young, but he was younger — was with David Zinman. He came up to me and said, "Mr. Graffman, I have both your recordings of the Prokofiev. Just tell me if there is anything I should be aware of." So that is what happens when you get older than the conductor.

Q. Did you find many differences between Ormandy and Muti in their personalities, their rehearsal practices, and their conducting techniques?

A. Well, I played only once with Muti — the Ravel. They had very different personalities, of course, but this really had nothing to do with my going on stage and playing with them. I was not present for rehearsals other than my own. As for their conducting techniques, Ormandy seemed more involved in sounds – sound for the sake of sound – more like a Rubinstein or Horowitz approach to the piano, as opposed to Serkin's more formal architectural approach. Not that the two conductors did not have both aspects, but they had different emphases that you could recognize.

Q. You played many times at the Robin Hood Dell and the Mann Center as well as at the Academy. Is there a great difference in playing in such distinct venues?

A. Playing out-of-doors has its difficulties. One time with Sixten Ehrling, the Swedish conductor, we began three different times with Tchaikovsky's Second. The first time we were five minutes into the concerto when it started to rain, and the concert was called off. The second time, on the next day, it was already raining, so the entire concert was canceled. On the third attempt, we were able to play it.

For outdoor concerts you have only one rehearsal. I remember at the Robin Hood Dell – the Ravel – where there are two long cadenzas. Just before the rehearsal, the conductor asked if I wanted to play these cadenzas. I suspect he was hoping that I would not, because of the time element. But I wanted to hear the piano, so I played the cadenzas and we stopped twice. It meant that I took 22 minutes instead of the allotted 20. This is the normal way of proceeding for a summer concert.

Q. Do you think the Orchestra still has the Philadelphia sound?

A. Yes, in spite of Muti and Sawallisch, and now Eschenbach, three great conductors who put their own individual stamp on the music. But the original sound is there, a lush, gorgeous sound, especially with the incredible strings, but not only with the strings, with everything. There is no conductor, in my opinion, who does not want to employ this sound, and wallow in it. As Muti was the first conductor after Ormandy, any changes were noticed immediately. After 44 years with Ormandy, there was suddenly someone new. And now there have been two more conductors after Muti, each with his own interpretation. But the sound is still there, as I said.

Q. Turning to the association of these three maestros with the Curtis Institute of Music: how did the students react to these conductors?

A. I was not here during Ormandy's years. That is, I studied at Curtis from age seven to 17, from 1936 to 1946.

As a student, I was not involved with conducting classes. Then came my concerts. I really did not hear or know how the students reacted to Ormandy. He was involved with Curtis when Rudolf Serkin was the director. It was Stokowski who was involved with the beginning of Curtis. He told Mary Louise Curtis Bok that he and Josef Hofmann would participate in this new school if it would be tuition-free. Hofmann became the director, and Stokowski was in charge of the orchestra. Stokowski had an ulterior motive. He wanted to get a reservoir of players for his orchestra because, up to that time, the conductors of great orchestras would go to Europe for the players. In a short period, say from five to eight years, this flow from Curtis to the Philadelphia Orchestra began, which is still continuing today. The Orchestra has become almost 50 percent Curtis graduates.

Ormandy was on the faculty of Curtis and actually taught classes, but Muti did not. Because of his many other conducting commitments, he was not as available as Ormandy. Then when I became the director – well, in the summer before I officially started – I was in Venice, and Muti called me and said he would like to have some relationship with Curtis. Of course this was very good for Curtis. It meant that he was extremely nice if any of our conducting students wanted to sit in on his rehearsals with the Philadelphia Orchestra. Physically he came and rehearsed about once a year at Curtis.

Sawallisch also came about once a year, although in one season he conducted a concert at the Academy of Music with the Curtis Orchestra.

Guest conductors often come to Curtis. Simon Rattle comes every time he is here, but he conducts in Philadelphia only every two years. David Zinman has come four or five times to conduct our Orchestra in the Academy, and recently in Verizon Hall.

Of course the students are delighted with these experiences, not only because of the advantage of playing with these great conductors, but because it is something new for them.

Q. In your opinion, what were the most important contributions of each of the three maestros?

A. Every conductor has something to offer that is unique. He must give a convincing performance which leaves the impression, while it is going on, that this is the only way to play that particular piece. It is the combination of sound, architecture, and the impact of how you build up climaxes which may be quite different for different conductors. Ormandy has made the contribution of sound – his wonderful gift of sound. Muti concentrated on the form of the piece. Sawallisch is especially impressive in the great Viennese-German repertoire: Mozart, Haydn, Beethoven, Schubert, as well as Strauss. All three are great conductors.

Interview with L A N G L A N G

Pianist

Q. You made your Philadelphia Orchestra debut in the Academy of Music in May 2001, with Music Director Wolfgang Sawallisch, and you appeared again with Sawallisch and the Orchestra in December 2001.[2] How would you describe the manner in which Maestro Sawallisch collaborates with the soloist?

A. I must say that I enjoyed playing the concertos with him very much, both times. I also played the Grieg Concerto with Maestro Sawallisch in Philadelphia, in January of 2003. He is a wonderful musician with great tradition.

Q. Did you find distinctive characteristics in Mr. Sawallisch's rehearsal technique?

A. He has such excellent hands. Well, he's really a great musician, and in the rehearsal you feel this. He doesn't speak a lot, but everything he says is so exact, and everything really works right away.

Q. In June 2001, during the Orchestra's hundredth-anniversary tour of Asia, you joined Maestro Sawallisch and the Orchestra in Beijing, playing the Mendelssohn Concerto. Was it different to be on tour with Sawallisch than it was to play a single concert?

A. No. He is just the same. He has a phenomenal power. I must say that Maestro Sawallisch looks wonderful, with such a youthful face. He has such bright color and such smooth skin. I guess he goes to those spa places in Germany during the summers. I think he knows how to rest.

That was such an exciting time for me, the first time to be playing with an American orchestra in my native country.

Q. In spite of your youth, you have already performed with almost every major orchestra. How do the differing personalities of the conductors affect the relationship between soloist and conductor? Does working with different conductors change your interpretation of a composition?

A. Sometimes conductors really have a very big influence on you. It's really hard to say. It depends on what orchestra you are playing with. Sometimes you get the right orchestra and the right conductor, and you, the pianist, need to be right, too. I don't change my interpretation, but sometimes I get inspired by great musicians and I play better. A great conductor brings you to a different level of playing.

Q Does the soloist have the final word, or are you obliged to follow the conductor's ways?

A. You need always to be fair with the music. For me, sometimes the tempos are hard to know because a conductor has different tempos marked. With Sawallisch, there were never any problems. Everything was wonderful.

Q. You sometimes add an encore after your concerto, which, of course, delights the audience but is quite unusual. Are most conductors, including Maestro Sawallisch, amenable to the addition?

A. You are talking about America. In Europe it is totally natural to play an encore. In America the time is ruled by the union. I mean, an encore adds time. I know this, and so in America I sometimes don't keep this tradition. Anyway, sometimes I feel inspired and if the audience wants it, I like to give a little surprise. Of course, I need to play something very short; otherwise

I will need to pay the orchestra. Mr. Sawallisch was always amenable to an encore, since he was used to it in Germany.

Q. As a student at Curtis, did you come in contact with Maestro Sawallisch?

A. Occasionally he came to Curtis for rehearsals. Being at Curtis, and around the Philadelphia Orchestra, introduced me to Maestro Sawallisch.

Q. Is there anything else that you would like to add about Mr. Sawallisch and the Orchestra?

A. Of course, I came in the later years of Mr. Sawallisch's directorship of the Orchestra. I want to say what a superb musician he is. The Orchestra, with him, is always in good condition. They have wonderful chemistry together. Maestro Sawallisch is so very well liked by the musicians, and it is such a good thing that he is coming back to conduct.

The Philadelphia Orchestra is very special in my career and in my life. I consider it my home orchestra. I love to play with this Orchestra, especially because there are lots of musicians from Curtis – so many of my friends – and I feel so close to them. It is a wonderful feeling to play with so many friends. Now that Maestro Eschenbach is here, I also like very much to make music with him and the Orchestra.

Roberto Diaz, one of my friends in the Orchestra, will be the new director of Curtis. He is a wonderful guy and an outstanding musician. I am sad at Mr. Graffman leaving Curtis, but at the same time I am happy that Roberto will take over. It was an excellent decision to have Roberto on board, and Curtis must be proud to have him.

I want to add that I love Maestro Sawallisch very much, very much. I wish him good health, and I hope that it is good all the time. He is such a profound musician and a great, great person, and I admire that.

Interview with S A R A H   C H A N G

Violinist

Q. You made your Philadelphia debut with Riccardo Muti and the Philadelphia Orchestra in January of 1991, when you were 10 years old. You played the first movement of Paganini's Violin Concerto No. 1. Could you describe how Muti dealt with such a young soloist?

A. I auditioned for Maestro Muti when I was eight. I had never done an audition before. Norman Carol, the concertmaster, was my support system and basically was there to hold my hand. He told me that Maestro Muti was wary of the whole process of auditions and competitions. But after the audition, Maestro Muti asked me if I would be available for a gala concert at the Academy in January of 1991. So by the actual concert, I had just turned 10. Since there was so much on the program, the selections for each performer were about 10 minutes, which is the reason that I played only the first movement of the Paganini. The gala was a spectacular, gorgeous concert, so exciting. Maestro Muti's kindness to me gave a huge jump start to my career, for which I am very grateful.

Q. In October of 1993, two years later, you played the entire Paganini Violin Concerto with Wolfgang Sawallisch and the Orchestra. Did you find it very different to play with Maestro Sawallisch?

A. They have extremely different personalities. Maestro Muti is a flamboyant Italian. Maestro Sawallisch has an authoritative great force. They have very different ways of rehearsing. Usually rehearsals are very informal, and everybody dresses in jeans or other casual outfits. You are there to work. But Maestro Sawallisch has proper rehearsals. I know that this is superficial, but when I walked in for my first rehearsal with Maestro Sawallisch, I was amazed because he was perfectly dressed in a three-piece suit and tie, something I had never seen in a rehearsal. I asked him if he had come from a wedding, or an interview. The administration people were hiding their eyes and trying not to laugh, and later they said to me, "Sarah, he always dresses like that." I love this Old World charm and the elegance he brings to all rehearsals and performances. It makes everybody sit up straighter.

Q. You recorded a CD with Sawallisch in 1993 at Memorial Hall in Fairmount Park.[3] How difficult was it to play in that hall?

A. Most of my recording is done in Europe. In Memorial Hall I remember looking around, and it was a basketball court, for crying out loud, with hoops at either end. I played facing the scoreboard. Also the control room was very far away, and since I like to hear the playbacks, I think I lost at least five pounds by constantly running there and back again. It was one of the most interesting venues that I have ever played in. But it was fun. I was happy to be recording with my home orchestra and in Philadelphia.

Q. 1993 was Sawallisch's first year as music director. Seven years later you played the Sarasate Fantasy on Bizet's *Carmen* at the one-hundredth anniversary concert,

November 16, 2000. By this time had you established a warm rapport with the maestro?

A. By 2000 Maestro Sawallisch and I had played together many times. Every time you are with a musical partner, you become more comfortable. You mold a relationship together. You get to know what he likes, what he doesn't like, and what your own preferences are. Playing together brings you closer together as musicians, and the circle tightens. Every working experience with Maestro Sawallisch was such a pleasure, and I think we developed a good relationship.

Among our many performances, I remember particularly the 1998 concert at the Core State Stadium to celebrate the fiftieth anniversary of the founding of Israel. Zubin Mehta was on one side with the Israel Philharmonic, and Wolfgang Sawallisch and the Philadelphia Orchestra on the other. Backstage was so much fun. We had Tony Bennett and Kathleen Battle and others. It was so cool. We were in a hockey stadium, and all rules flew out the window. Until the night before the concert, they had not decided which orchestra I was to solo with, but it was fitting that I play with my home orchestra. To his astonishment, Maestro Sawallisch learned that he was to be paired with a jazz group and that he and the Orchestra were to accompany them in three or four numbers. And he did beautifully. I love events like this, because I play so many subscription concerts, and this is different.

Q. Also in 2000 you recorded a CD of Strauss's Concerto for Violin and Orchestra in D Minor, with Sawallisch and the Bavarian Radio Symphony Orchestra, plus the Sonata for Violin and Piano by Strauss, with Sawallisch as the pianist. Is there a similarity between Sawallisch the conductor and Sawallisch the pianist?

A. The overall musicality of Maestro Sawallisch is the same, with his ideas and phrasing – it is all magical. I love to play chamber music with him. Somehow you seem to come closer together as musicians.

The CD was released in 2000, but we made this recording a year earlier, when I was 18. Maestro Sawallisch is a beautiful pianist and a Strauss master. We had been playing the Strauss Sonata here and there since I was 12. Then he asked me if I knew this Strauss Concerto – which hardly anyone plays – and he told me to take a look at it, that it was a lovely youthful work. I think we always had it back in our minds to record the Sonata some day, and then the Strauss Concerto for Violin and Orchestra just fit perfectly in the CD.

Q. I have noted several programs in which you have played the same composition with different conductors. Do their different personalities affect the soloist?

A. Absolutely. It makes all the difference in the world. Playing with different conductors is like approaching a completely fresh, new piece, even if it's a piece that you've played 600 times, like a concerto by Tchaikovsky, Mendelssohn, or Brahms, stuff like that. (Actually, I probably have played them 600 times.) With different conductors, you constantly learn new things, which motivates me. I know that some artists think that you play the same regardless of who is conducting, but I find that working with different conductors really has a huge amount of influence on me in keeping the music fresh and interesting every time I play. After all, we are not machines.

Q. You donated your talent in a concert in Philadelphia to benefit the Chaim Medical Center in Tel Hashomer, Israel. This was a project that Mrs. Sawallisch began before her death. Did Maestro Sawallisch take part in the concert?

A. Yes, he was the pianist. Mrs. Sawallisch was an absolutely amazing person, and I was crushed when I learned of her death. I was playing in London, and Maestro Sawallisch called and asked me to play at his wife's memorial service in Munich. I jetted over for three hours and played the second movement of Bach's Violin Concerto, with Zubin Mehta conducting the Deutsche Symphony. It was such a touchingly beautiful service.

Q. As a soloist, what would you say were the greatest strengths of Muti and of Sawallisch?

A. I think that Maestro Muti brought energy to the Orchestra, and a fresh approach to many things. Maestro Sawallisch brought back Old School depth.

Any concert for me with the Philadelphia Orchestra has a special place in my heart because it is my home orchestra.

NOTES

Chapter One: Eugene Ormandy

[1] Herbert Kupferberg, "The Ormandy Era," in *The Philadelphia Orchestra: A Century of Music*, ed. John Ardoin (Philadelphia: Temple University Press, 1999) 79.

[2] The announcement was released on September 29, 1938, and is quoted by Oliver Daniel, *Stokowski: A Counterpoint of View* (New York: Dodd, Mead & Company, 1982) 343.

[3] His mother's name may have been Rosalie Ormandy Blau.

[4] Hope Stoddard, *Symphony Conductors of the U.S.A.* (New York: Thomas Crowell Company, 1957) 148.

[5] David Ewen, ed., *Musicians Since 1900: Performers in Concert and Opera* (New York: H. Wilson Co., 1978) 599.

[6] Daniel, *Stokowski,* 373–74.

[7] The sound was helped by the quality of the string instruments that the Orchestra owned. Ormandy gave his Balestrieri violin and Tourte bow to the Orchestra to be used by the musicians.

[8] Kupferberg, "The Ormandy Era," 82.

[9] Herbert Kupferberg, *Those Fabulous Philadelphians: The Life and Times of a Great Orchestra* (New York: Charles Scribner's Sons, 1969) 132.

Vladimir Horowitz had great admiration for Ormandy as a Rachmaninoff specialist. When he recorded Rachmaninoff's

Piano Concerto No. 3, in live performance with the New York Philharmonic (1978), he insisted that Ormandy be invited to conduct.

10 Ewen, *Musicians Since 1900*, 601.

11 Kupferberg, *Those Fabulous Philadelphians*, 165.

12 Donald Brook, *International Gallery of Conductors* (London: Rockliff, 1951) 129.

13 Kupferberg, *Those Fabulous Philadelphians*, 149.

14 Ibid., 136.

15 Oliver Daniel disputes the idea that Ormandy promoted an invitation. He quotes the composer Richard Yardumian: "Ormandy did not want Stokowski in Philadelphia. It was the Board that wanted him." *Stokowski*, 692.

16 Bosley Crowther, "Night Song," *New York Times*, January 29, 1948.

17 Edward Arian, *Bach, Beethoven, and Bureaucracy: The Case of the Philadelphia Orchestra* (University, Alabama: University of Alabama Press, 1971) 27.

18 The musicians' working conditions and pay scale improved constantly. When Ormandy took over the Orchestra, they had only a 28-week contract. After the 1961 strike, the season was extended to 35 weeks. In 1963 they gained a 52-week employment contract, but the policy of compulsory retirement at age 65 persisted for several years.

19 Only Frederick Stock of the Chicago Symphony came close to Ormandy's long tenure. Stock became assistant conductor in 1899 and was conductor from 1906 to 1942.

[20] Kupferberg, *Those Fabulous Philadelphians*, 145.

[21] Ormandy was a small man and apparently quite sensitive about this. Gretel took great pains to avoid being seen or photographed immediately next to him.

[22] Gretel Ormandy died in 1998. In her will she bequeathed $10 million, in both their names, to the Philadelphia Orchestra.

[23] Harold Schonberg is particularly critical of Ormandy's conducting and his place among conductors: *The Great Conductors* (New York: Simon and Schuster, 1967) 340.

[24] New EMI reissues, in the company's prestigious *Great Conductors of the 20th Century* series, feature many Ormandy releases. See David Patrick Stearns, "Stokowski, Ormandy, Muti: Rereleases, Reassessments," *Philadelphia Inquirer,* September 3, 2002.

Chapter Two: Riccardo Muti

[1] Herbert Kupferberg, *Those Fabulous Philadelphians: The Life and Times of a Great Orchestra* (New York: Charles Scribner's Sons, 1969) 193–94.

[2] Matthew Gurewitsch, "A Man of Essences," in *Riccardo Muti: Twenty Years in Philadelphia,* ed. Judith Kurnick (Philadelphia: Philadelphia Orchestra Association, 1992) 17.

[3] Before Muti's appointment as music director, Ormandy announced to the Orchestra during a rehearsal that Claudio

Abbado had been offered the position of music director, but that he had declined. (Reported by a musician in the Orchestra who was present for this announcement.)

4 Comment excerpted in Philip Hart, *Conductors: A New Generation* (New York: Charles Scribner's Sons, 1979) 124.

5 Matthew Gurewitsch, "The Muti Era," in *The Philadelphia Orchestra: A Century of Music*, ed. John Ardoin (Philadelphia: Temple University Press, 1999) 141.

6 Helena Matheopou, *Maestros: Encounters with Conductors Today* (London: Hutchinson, 1982) 375.

7 Gurewitsch, "The Muti Era," 136.

8 Ibid., 130.

9 *Tosca* was the first Muti-Philadelphia concert opera to be recorded. Originally they recorded the opera in the Academy of Music, putting 55 microphones on the stage. Then, for better sound, they took this recording to a church in Holland and re-recorded it there. The same procedure was used for *Pagliacci.* Daniel Webster, "Muti in the Recording Studio," in *Riccardo Muti: Twenty Years in Philadelphia*, 26.

10 Norman Lebrecht, *The Maestro Myth: Guest Conductors in Pursuit of Power* (New York: Simon & Schuster, 1991) 225.

11 Muti has recorded with the Philadelphia Orchestra, the Philharmonia and the New Philharmonia, the Berlin Philharmonic, La Scala Orchestra, the London Philharmonic, the Vienna Philharmonic, the Orchestra of the Maggio Musicale Fiorentino, the Orchestra of Covent Garden, the Bavarian Orchestra, the RAI Symphony Orchestra of Milan, RAI of Rome, RAI of Naples, and RAI Scarlatti of Naples.

12 David Patrick Stearns, "Stokowski, Ormandy, Muti: Rereleases, Reassessments," *Philadelphia Inquirer*, September 3, 2002.

13 Lebrecht, *The Maestro Myth*, 223.

14 Hart, *Conductors*, 109.

15 Lebrecht, *The Maestro Myth*, 226.

16 There is a touching tribute from Gretel Ormandy: "I am sad that your time in Philadelphia was so short. But we also knew from the beginning that the world would be beckoning. However, this is not goodbye. You will be coming back." Music director-designate Wolfgang Sawallisch expressed his gratitude and congratulations.

17 Peter Dobrin, "Sawallisch Is Frail, but Musically Mighty," *Philadelphia Inquirer*, January 10, 2004.

18 "For Muti, Years Advance but Greatness Recedes," July 29, 2001.

19 "The Brahms Glowed, and Muti Did, Too," *Philadelphia Inquirer*, February 15, 2005.

20 Quoted by David Patrick Stearns, "Muti Resigns Directorship at La Scala Opera," *Philadelphia Inquirer*, April 3, 2005.

Chapter Three: Wolfgang Sawallisch

1 Barrymore Laurence Scherer, "The Sawallisch Era," in *The Philadelphia Orchestra: A Century of Music*, ed. John Ardoin (Philadelphia: Temple University Press, 1999) 198–99.

2 *Im Interesse der Deutlichkeit: Mein Leben mit der Musik* (Hamburg: Hoffmann und Campe Vertag, 1988).

3 "Sawallisch Discovers America," February 16, 1964.

4 Michael Elkin, "Who Is Sawallisch?" November 28, 1993.

5 Early in his career, Sawallisch was reluctant to conduct *Missa Solemnis* because he felt that he had not found the essential key. In 1970 he was asked to perform it at the Vatican in honor of the two-hundredth anniversary of Beethoven's birth and the tenth anniversary of Pope Paul VI's pontificate. He called it one of the high points of his life, despite the struggle between the great architecture of St. Peter's Basilica and the eight-second reverberation.

6 Robert Driver, artistic director of the Philadelphia Opera Company, invited Maestro Sawallisch to conduct an opera, but he declined. On another occasion, Sawallisch stated that he had conducted more than twelve hundred operas with the Bavarian State Opera, and it was enough.

7 Paul Horsley, "Sawallisch's American Adventure," in *The Philadelphia Orchestra Celebrates Sawallisch,* ed. Sedgwick Clark (Philadelphia: Philadelphia Orchestra Association, 2003) 19.

8 Sawallisch's first performance at the German Society occurred when he was guest-conducting the Orchestra in 1986. At a 2001 concert, the president of the German Society told the audience that Mechthild Sawallisch had confided to him that their move to Philadelphia was the best decision they had ever made.

9 B. L. Scherer, "A Noble Legacy," in *The Philadelphia Orchestra Celebrates Sawallisch,* 30.

[10] Penderecki's Piano Concerto was commissioned by Carnegie Hall for Emanuel Ax and the Philadelphia Orchestra.

[11] Sawallisch donated the prize money to the Curtis Institute of Music.

[12] In addition to the Philadelphia Orchestra, Sawallisch has recorded with the Berlin Philharmonic, the London Philharmonic, the Royal Concertgebouw Orchestra, the Philharmonia Orchestra, RAI Orchestra, the Vienna Symphony, Orchestra della Suizzera Italiana, Bayerisches Staatsorchester, Staatskapelle Dresden, and the Bavarian Radio Symphony.

[13] In 1997 local radio broadcasts were resumed on WFLN (subsequently WRTI). In 1997–98 there were 13 weeks of nationally syndicated broadcasts.

[14] This DVD has an added interview with Sawallisch. In one part he discusses the difference between German–European symphonies, supported by the state, and American symphony orchestras, supported by the private sector. He speaks with enthusiasm about the interdependence of the American orchestra and its audiences, and ends with the opinion that the two systems are beginning to come closer.

[15] In one of his last interviews as music director, Sawallisch stated: "The Philadelphia Orchestra is, in my opinion, the crowning position of all the music director possibilities in the world." David Patrick Stearns, "In Maestro's Words, Tumult and Triumphs of Philadelphia Tenure," *Philadelphia Inquirer*, April 27, 2003.

[16] Brian S. Atwood, "Meet the Philadelphia Orchestra," in *The Philadelphia Orchestra: One Hundredth Birthday Salute,* commemorative book (November 16, 2000) 27.

[17] Lesley Valdés, "Sawallisch, the Man, the Maestro, the Widower," *Philadelphia Inquirer,* February 28, 1999.

[18] *Im Interesse der Deutlichkeit: Mein Leben mit der Musik,* 228.

[19] Cardinal Josef Ratzinger (now Pope Benedict XVI) celebrated a memorial mass in the Munich Cathedral. Sawallisch is a Lutheran, but the cardinal was a personal friend and Mechthild Sawallisch was a Catholic. Sawallisch donated $3 million to the Orchestra from his wife's estate. A CD, *Nature's Realm,* is dedicated to her memory. Sawallisch's final three concerts were sponsored by the Mechthild Sawallisch Fund for Gifted Female Vocalists.

[20] Eckhart Schmidt, "On Searching for the Holy Grail," in *The Philadelphia Orchestra Celebrates Sawallisch,* 25.

[21] Peter Dobrin, "Sawallisch and Sure Hand Return," February 12, 2005. The reviewer adds: "It is only under Sawallisch that the Philadelphia Orchestra sounds like the Philadelphia Orchestra."

[22] Anthony Tommasini, "In Praise of the Youthful Codgers," February 1, 2004.

Chapter Four: Voices from the Music World

[1] In 1947, the Tchaikovsky Concertos 2 and 3, which he then recorded right after the performances; in 1965, the

Rhapsody on a Theme of Paganini, by Rachmaninoff; in 1967, the Grieg Concerto in A Major; in 1968, Tchaikovsky Concerto No. 2 – all in Philadelphia. In 1971, the Brahms Concerto No. 1 in B Flat, on tour in Ames, Iowa; in 1977, Rachmaninoff 2 in Philadelphia, in New York, and at the Ann Arbor May Festival.

2 Mendelssohn, Piano Concerto No. 1, Op. 25 (May); Prokofiev, Piano Concerto No. 3 in C Major, Op. 26 (December).

3 On EMI: Paganini Op. 6 and Saint-Saens: *Havanaise for Violin and Orchestra,* and Introduction and *Rondo Capriccioso for Violin and Orchestra*, Op. 28.

SELECTED BIBLIOGRAPHY

Arian, Edward. *Bach, Beethoven, and Bureaucracy: The Case of the Philadelphia Orchestra.* University, Alabama: University of Alabama Press, 1971.

Baldwin, Lou. "Sawallisch Reflects on Religious Influences on Music." *Catholic Standard & Times*, February 11, 1999. P. 29.

Bamberger, Carl. *The Conductor's Art.* New York: McGraw-Hill, 1965.

Brook, Donald. *International Gallery of Conductors.* London: Rocklift, 1951.

Crowther, Bosley. "Night Song." *New York Times*, January 29, 1948.

Daniel, Oliver. *Stokowski: A Counterpoint of View.* New York: Dodd, Mead & Company, 1982.

Di Nardo, Tom. "Sawallisch, on 'Solemnis.'" *Daily News*, February 1, 2001.

Dobrin, Peter. "The Brahms Glowed, and Muti Did, Too." *Philadelphia Inquirer,* February 15, 2005.

————. "For Sawallisch, No Slower Tempo." *Philadelphia Inquirer,* January 27, 2002.

————. "Sawallisch and Sure Hand Return." *Philadelphia Inquirer*, February 12, 2005.

————. "Sawallisch Is Frail, but Musically Mighty." *Philadelphia Inquirer,* January 10, 2004.

————. "Tchaikovsky Symphony No. 6 'Pathetique.' Orchestre National de France Conducted by Riccardo Muti." *Philadelphia Inquirer,* August 29, 2004.

Elkin, Michael. "Who Is Sawallisch?" *Jewish Exponent,* November 26, 1993. P. 34.

Ewen, David, ed. *Musicians Since 1900: Performers in Concert and Opera.* New York: H. Wilson Co., 1978.

Green, Elizabeth A. *The Modern Conductor.* Upper Saddle River, N.J.: Prentice Hall, 1997.

Gurewitsch, Matthew. "A Man of Essences." In *Riccardo Muti: Twenty Years in Philadelphia,* ed. Judith Kurnick. Philadelphia: Philadelphia Orchestra Association, 1992.

————. "The Muti Era." In *The Philadelphia Orchestra: A Century of Music,* ed. John Ardoin, 126–41. Philadelphia: Temple University Press, 1999.

Hart, Philip. *Conductors: A New Generation.* New York: Charles Scribner's Sons, 1979.

Horsley, Paul. "Sawallisch's American Adventure." In *The Philadelphia Orchestra Celebrates Sawallisch,* ed. Sedgwick Clark, 14–21. Philadelphia: Philadelphia Orchestra Association, 2003.

Johnson, Stephen. "Old Sound, New Resonance." *New York Times,* September 19, 1993.

Klein, Howard. "Sawallisch Discovers America." *New York Times*, February 16, 1964.

Kruckenberg, Sven. *The Symphony Orchestra and Its Instruments*. Gothenburg, Sweden: Chartwell Books, 2002.

Kupferberg, Herbert. "The Ormandy Era." In *The Philadelphia Orchestra: A Century of Music*, ed. John Ardoin, 72–91. Philadelphia: Temple University Press, 1999.

————. *Those Fabulous Philadelphians: The Life and Times of a Great Orchestra*. New York: Charles Scribner's Sons, 1969.

Lebrecht, Norman. *The Maestro Myth: Guest Conductors in Pursuit of Power*. New York: Simon & Schuster, 1991.

Matheopou, Helena. *Maestros: Encounters with Conductors Today*. London: Hutchinson, 1982.

Ormandy, Eugene. Oral History Collection. Rare Book and Manuscript Library, University of Pennsylvania. Philadelphia, Pa.

Polisi, Joseph W. *The Artist as Citizen*. Pompton Plains, N.J.: Amadeus Press, 2005.

Sawallisch, Wolfgang. *Im Interesse der Deutlichkeit: Mein Leben mit der Musik*. Hamburg: Hoffmann und Campe Vertag, 1988.

Scherer, Barrymore Laurence. "A Noble Legacy." In *The Philadelphia Orchestra Celebrates Sawallisch*, ed. Sedgwick Clark, 26–35. Philadelphia: Philadelphia Orchestra Association, 2003.

————. "The Sawallisch Era." In *The Philadelphia Orchestra: A Century of Music*, ed. John Ardoin, 192–209. Philadelphia: Temple University Press, 1999.

Schmidt, Eckhart. "On Searching for the Holy Grail." In *The Philadelphia Orchestra Celebrates Sawallisch*, ed. Sedgwick Clark, 23–25. Philadelphia: Philadelphia Orchestra Association, 2003.

Schonberg, Harold. *The Great Conductors*. New York: Simon and Schuster, 1967.

Stearns, David Patrick. "For Muti, Years Advance but Greatness Recedes." *Philadelphia Inquirer*, July 29, 2001.

————. "In Maestro's Words, Tumult and Triumphs of Philadelphia Tenure." *Philadelphia Inquirer*, April 27, 2003.

————. "Muti Resigns Directorship at La Scala Opera." *Philadelphia Inquirer*, April 3, 2005.

————. "Stokowski, Ormandy, Muti: Rereleases, Reassessments." *Philadelphia Inquirer*, September 3, 2002.

Stoddard, Hope. *Symphony Conductors of the U.S.A.* New York: Thomas Crowell Company, 1957.

Tommasini, Anthony. "In Praise of the Youthful Codgers." *New York Times*, February 1, 2004.

Valdés, Lesley. "Sawallisch, the Man, the Maestro, the Widower." *Philadelphia Inquirer*, February 28, 1999.

Webster, Daniel. "Muti in the Recording Studio." In *Riccardo Muti: Twenty Years in Philadelphia*, ed. Judith Kurnick. Philadelphia: Philadelphia Orchestra Association, 1992.

INDEX

PHYLLIS WHITE RODRÍGUEZ-PERALTA is an Emeritus Professor of Temple University, formerly the Chair of the Department of Spanish and Portuguese. She is the author of *José Santos Chocano: An Analysis of His Works*, and *Tres poetas cumbres en la poesía peruana: Chocano, Eguren y Vallejo*.